WOMAN'S WRONGS:

A COUNTER-IRRITANT.

BY

GAIL HAMILTON.

"Si quid novisti rectius istis,
Candidus imperti; si non, his utere mecum."

BOSTON:
TICKNOR AND FIELDS.
1868.

University Press: Welch, Bigelow, & Co.,
Cambridge.

WOMAN'S WRONGS.

THE friendliness existing between women and clergymen, though not usually considered especially complimentary to either class, is a matter of common recognition. It is generally referred to with a certain half-bantering condescension, that sometimes scarcely stops short of a sneer. Yet this friendliness is in part, at least, founded on a law of human nature which it is not wise to overlook. Clergymen, whatever may be their theories about woman, are forced by the very exigencies of their profession to treat women as independent human beings. The teachings and the example of the Divine Master are too plain to be misinterpreted, and the issues too momentous to be neglected. The clergyman more than any other looks at woman from the pure point of soul. He knows that, notwithstanding all the dictates of conventional propriety, truth and nature, in supreme interests, assert their sway; and a woman's soul is to him just as self-centred, just as responsible, just as important, as a man's soul. All talk of incompleteness and dependence, of oaks and vines, is hushed before the Divine voice: "If thou be wise, thou shalt be wise for thyself; but if thou scornest, thou alone shalt bear it."

When this voice finds no echo in the clergyman's soul; when this respect is simply conventional, enforced by the requirements of his profession, active only in one direction, having no influence over his every-day opinions; when his spirit is not elevated by the language he uses, by the air he breathes, — he sinks lower than his fellows. The very fact that he can resist such influences indicates a soul indissolubly wedded to earthliness, and we may confidently count on finding a conscience insensible to appeal, conceit impenetrable to facts, a sensuality incapable of purification, a character beyond reclamation.

The Rev. John Todd, D. D. has lately been moved to announce and expound the laws of human life, especially in their bearing upon the relations between man and woman. He has done so with a wisdom accurately described by James in the fifteenth verse of the third chapter of his Epistle. If to diminish disgust of vice, and to destroy the charm of innocence, be success, he has indeed achieved a singular success. He turned his attention to a thing,

> " Horrible, hateful, monstrous, not to be told,"

and he so managed to overlay it with impotent and sometimes ridiculous logic, with ill-directed denunciation, with irreverent assumption of Divine prerogatives, with Scriptural misrepresentations, with a kind of talk for which the popular phrase "silly sentimentalism" is too substantial, and which is better described by sentimental silliness, that pious fatuity did the work of infernal cleverness, and the original offence seemed likely to escape its just condemnation through scorn of the folly and immorality directed against it. He touched a sacrament, and it shrivelled into profanity. Marriage became in his hands a base commercial transaction. Woman was reduced to the level of the beasts that perish. What is beyond the province of reasoning he did not scruple to force under the yoke of his sophistry. Things secret and sacred, the soul's most solemn symbolism, God's own trust to the hidden heart of humanity, too deep, too holy, too awful for sound, or sight, or touch, he brought out remorselessly to the blare of argument, and the glare of ambition, and the stare of stupidity.

Through the rank growths of selfishness his words spread like prairie fire. A gospel that preaches masculine self-gratification as manly religion, the lowest womanly subserviency to man as the sole womanly way of doing God service, is not the boon of every day, nor to be lightly let slip. Its improbabilities, its inconsistencies, its monstrosities, seemed to go down sweetly, like the grapes of Beulah. Clerical conferences passed resolutions fortifying Dr. Todd's position. "Religious" newspapers hastened to give him their sanction. Secular newspapers became suddenly devout, and, ranging themselves by the side of their religious brethren, went singing Te Deums after Dr. Todd. The piety of it, Iago, the piety of it! Liberal Christian and bigoted Puritan, man of God and man of the world, all who loved themselves better than righteousness, who would rejoice to see iniquity framed into a moral law and transmuted into gospel, — all, for once, laid down the weapons of their warfare, and joined in the holy shout, "There is no god but God, and Dr. Todd is his prophet!"

Into the region whither Dr. Todd thus betook himself it is not permitted to follow him. Over the new heaven and the new earth of his own creation he must hold undisputed sway. But whom the gods will destroy they first make mad. Deceived, probably, by the silence of those whose disapproval was not the less deep because unspoken, mistaking the noisy applause of selfishness and thoughtlessness for the verdict of virtue, he has ventured forth into a field where it is possible to meet him; he has put his hand to things which it is not desecration to handle; and I propose to take advantage of the opportunity which he has himself furnished to examine, for a few moments, the calibre of this man who has been so suddenly set up as a moral lawgiver to woman.

In late issues of an able, if not the leading, religious newspaper of New England, appeared a series of articles from the pen of Dr. Todd, entitled "Women's Rights." The newspaper thus recommends them: "The principles advanced and urged with the author's customary felicity of thought and expression are such, we think, as will meet the views of our readers." The same articles have just been published in book or pamphlet form — I have not seen the republication — by a Boston house; and an able, if not the leading, secular newspaper of New England declares the book to be "full of good strong common-sense, which will commend it to the great majority of American women." I have diligently examined the critical notices of the press, and have found this opinion echoed, East and West, with scarcely a dissenting voice. It is this essay to which I beg to call attention. The authority given it by its indorsers is my only apology for detaining the reader over assertions that are either baseless or purposeless, and arguments that have been a thousand times refuted.

Dr. Todd begins with a mixture of majesty and sweetness at once imposing and conciliating.

"Sound, as it goes from the bell in the church-tower, probably goes in waves and curves, and not in straight lines.

Human feeling and thought seem to move in tidal waves, modified, doubtless, by the peculiarities of the age. At one time the women of Rome became so discouraged and down-hearted with their condition, that they committed suicide to such an extent that the Senate, alarmed, passed a decree that all who should hereafter commit suicide should have their bodies exposed *naked* in the streets. The instincts of modesty came to woman's aid, and there were no more suicides. On the true instincts of the sex I rely, while I speak to the women of my generation kindly, faithfully, plainly, calmly, and decidedly."

The women of my generation must see at the outset that a new course is to be adopted towards them. They are no longer to be spoiled children. They are to come under a discipline gentle but firm, and be brought up in the way they should go.

But if Dr. Todd had searched through the world, he could hardly have found an historical illustration better adapted to his essay than the one he has chosen. It strikes the key-note of his thought. The women of Rome were so wretched that they rushed to death for relief. The Senate thereupon passed a decree, not to abate the wretchedness, but to prevent its expression; not to make life more attractive, but death more repulsive. After eighteen hundred years of Christianity, Dr. Todd can think of no more excellent way.

"Discouraged *and* down-hearted" is perhaps one of those felicities of expression which we are called on to admire. Repetition and contradiction of word and sentiment will be found to be Dr. Todd's especial felicity. So far as happiness consists in setting adjectives and pronouns adrift without any visible means of support, the following sentence must be conceded to be eminently blissful: "Among the other sex there is a wide-spread uneasiness, — a discontentment with woman's lot, impatient of its burdens, rebellious against its sufferings, an undefined hope of emancipation from the ordinary lot of humanity, by some great revolution, so that her condition will be entirely changed!"

"This feeling" — we quote now rather for the felicity of the thought than of the expression — "crops out in publicly ridiculing marriage, dwelling on its evils, raving about the tyranny of men, crying for the 'emancipation of women.'"

Dr. Todd can never be suspected of using language to conceal ideas. Does he mean to say that this wide-spread uneasiness has no just foundation? Does he mean that this discontentment is discontentment with that which should cause only contentment; that this impatience, or, to quote him more accurately, this "impatient" is an "impatient" of burdens Divinely appointed, the "rebellious" a "rebellious" against sufferings Divinely ordained? He speaks of a "hope of emancipation from the ordinary lot of humanity"; what does he mean by "the ordinary lot of humanity"? Work and disease and death are the ordinary lot of humanity. Do women, in their worst conventions, demand from men emancipation from work, from disease and death, in their season? In the very next paragraph he says: "The demand is .... that .... women .... shall be educated as he [man] is, enter the same pursuits that he does, receive the same wages, occupy the same posts and professions, wield the same influence, and, in a word, be independent of man." Does that look like claiming exemption from the ordinary lot of humanity? Is it not rather a claim to share the ordinary lot of humanity?

In what Woman's Rights convention, from the pen of what Woman's Rights advocate, has Dr. Todd found any public ridicule of marriage, or any other dwelling on its evils than such as was intended to remove them?

Dr. Todd says: "The demand is, that .... she shall be allowed hereafter to be in all respects equal to man." Directly after he adds: "Nobody pretends that the sexes are equal in weight, in height, or in bodily strength." Does he mean that women demand the concession of an equality which they admit does not and cannot exist? His words say it. But it is not the "strong-minded women, who clamor and disgust their sex and ours in demanding 'women's rights,'" whom he addresses. He is wise in so doing. Women who had taken any thought for these things would speedily increase and intensify his disgust. It is to "those who shrink from these moral Camillas" that he sagaciously turns: "It is to this class of the sisterhood I am wishing to address myself at this time. Will you allow me, then, to come and sit down by your side, making no claim to superiority?" — dear, condescending man!

"Will you, will you, will you, will you walk in, Mr. Fly."

So far it is preface and introduction. Having comfortably established himself by the side of his "fair ones," he proceeds to treat of the equality of the sexes, on which he rashly promises to waste no words. This promise is fulfilled by making all the conventional concessions of woman's intuition, her delicacy of taste, the girl's quickness of mind up to a certain period as compared with the boy's.

"We, sons of dust, move slower, we creep, where you bound to the head of the stairs at a single leap." We must not pause to admire the grammatical felicity of "move slower," nor the rhetorical felicity of picturing women as mounting stairs *per saltum*, but go on to the finer felicities of thought. "'Why then,' my lady reader will say, '*why* can't we be independent of man?' for this is the gist of the whole subject. I reply, you can't for two reasons: first, God never designed you should; and secondly, your own deep instincts are in the way." From the manner in which the Divine designs and opinions are quoted by Dr. Todd, we should infer that the Almighty had taken that gentleman into his confidence. Certainly he speaks with a definiteness which ought to presuppose a new revelation of St. John the Divine. From the mere terrestrial point of view, we should say that his classification lies open to the charge of cross-division. Divine designs being indicated by human instincts, his first reason involves his second; but of course one who has the *entrée* of heaven is not dependent upon earthly facts for his knowledge. Familiarity, in his case, seems as usual to have bred contempt. He regards the Divine instrumentalities — these womanly instincts and limitations — quite insufficient to secure the desired end, and evidently believes that the Almighty could never accomplish his object with women unless the Rev. John Todd offered himself as a medium of communication. Accordingly, "bear with me, and keep good-natured, while I show you what you, dear ladies, cannot do, and God don't ask you to do.

"1. You cannot invent. There are all manner of inventions in our age, — steam, railroads, telegraphing, machinery of all kinds, often five hundred and fifty weekly applications for patents at the Patent Office, but among them all no female applicants." Here, felicities both of thought and expression crowd upon one another so rapidly that the "female mind" pauses bewildered. The invention of steam is a feat paralleled only by that of the young soldier who, when asked if Newburyport was his native place, said no, but on his return from the war he meant to make it so! Discriminating age, that invents applications, but not applicants; railroads and telegraphing, — a less felicitous writer might have said telegraphs, — but among them all no women!

"You have sewing-machines almost numberless, knitting-machines, washing, ironing, and churning machines; but I never heard of one that was the emanation of the female mind. Did you? . . . .

I suppose this power was denied you, lest it should take you out of your most important sphere, as I shall show."

"I suppose." So, then, Dr. Todd's revelation was fragmentary as well as that of St. Paul, who also was obliged to interpolate, "to the rest speak I, not the Lord."

It might be said, if the question were of invention, that possibly one reason why women have never been inventors is, that they have never been artisans; but the matter is utterly irrelevant. Granted that women cannot invent; granted that the sparrow killed cock-robin; — what of it? What connection is there between power of invention and woman's rights? Woman's rights means, perhaps chiefly, the right of suffrage. Does Dr. Todd maintain that inventive power is necessary to the possession or the exercise of that right? Does he mean to say that no man shall vote for town-officers till he has invented a sewing-machine? Of all the inventions of our age, — steam and telegraphing and female non-applicants, — I never heard of one that was the emanation of Dr. Todd's mind. Did you? Shall Dr. Todd therefore be disfranchised?

But, says Dr. Todd, with equal pertinence: "You cannot compete with men in a long course of mental labor. Your delicate organization never has and never can bear" (another happy grammatical touch) "the study by which you can become Newtons," and so forth. No woman has ever stood by the side of Phidias or Homer, and the girl's best training gives her less skill on the piano than her brother attains with no training at all.

Again, what of it? When Dr. Todd says so neatly, "And even in cooking and in millinery, as is well known, men must and do stand at the head of these occupations," we may infer from their superior fitness that millinery and cooking ought to be given up to men, — a proposition in which I should heartily concur; when he asks, "Did you ever know a woman who could endure being a teacher till seventy-five, as men often do?" we may say under the rose, "and might in some cases till seventy-five thousand, for all the fatigue their teaching need cause them"; but how does it all stand connected with "women's rights"? Do Newtons and Raphaels alone choose rulers and discern principles and pass judgment upon laws? How many Miltons and Canovas does Dr. Todd reckon in his congregation, and how cheerfully do the other members yield to them a political monopoly? If Dr. Todd should ever come to the conclusion that he cannot equal Shakespeare, will he at once propose to give up one third of his salary and his whole right of franchise?

"Delicate organization" is the alleged cause of this mental inability in woman, — "because her bodily organization cannot endure the pressure of continued and long labor as we can." She has "a peculiar organization, requiring the most careful and gentle treatment." How wide-spread is the evil which Dr. Todd deprecates? How many women in America are suffering from a mad endeavor to become Newtons and Raphaels, compared with the number who are straining every nerve, who are laboring to exhaustion, disease, and death, in the effort to earn their bread, to support helpless relatives, or, where there is not poverty, to do the every-day work of exacting households? How many female brains are exhausting themselves with a long course of severe mental labor, compared with the number that are destroying themselves by inaction? Dr. Todd is eager to snatch women from the gulf into which their strenuous intellectual work threatens to plunge them. He is painfully alive to the dangers that menace from Newton's Principia and Paradise Lost. He prescribes the most careful and gentle treatment to save women from the fatal effect of music and metaphysics; but of any hurtful demand upon female strength from other sources he seems to be entirely unaware. He recognizes no peculiarity or delicacy in the female organization, which incapacitates a woman for sewing all day, or standing behind a counter all day, or spending all day for weeks and years in doing, not household work merely, but household drudgery, with no holiday or holi-hour, but such as neutralizes itself by bringing increased toil in its train. Yet it seems impossible he should not know that, for one woman diseased by excessive brain-work, there are one hundred diseased by excessive nerve and muscle work or mental idleness. He has "no difficulty in admitting that the mind of woman is equal to ours, nay, if you please, superior." (This must be only one of Dr. Todd's "nice and pretty things." He cannot for a moment seriously harbor the suggestion that any female mind can really equal — *ours!*) It is her physical organization that stands in the way. His position then virtually is: The female mind is strong; the female body is weak: therefore the female mind must be spared, but the female body may be worked indefinitely. Q. E. D.

Dr. Todd says, with charming and elegant playfulness, "He is a poor dog that barks up the wrong tree, however loud or earnest he may bark," — a principle which, if truc, it is suicidal for him to enunciate.

"If what I have said," continues the unterrified Doctor, "seems to want gallantry, I reply, it is not gallantry that I am now after, but facts, — truth, — the true sphere and power and glory of woman." Not at all. One may ransack his whole essay in vain for a single indication that he is in search of truth, or facts, or woman's sphere. Everything goes to show that he considers himself already in possession of the truth; he is quite settled in his own mind as to what is really woman's sphere, and he is concerned only to bring women over to his way of thinking.

"Be patient. I have some nice and pretty things to say, some garlands to weave, after I have led you to see the great facts of your being." Not after I have discovered them, but after I have led you to see them. Take heart, dear ladies. You are not to be given over to uncovenanted mercies. Dr. Todd will take you tenderly by the hand, he will guide your wayward little feet to the abyss of your incapacity. But having given you a glimpse into its depths, and convinced you that, unlike your fathers and husbands, you cannot invent steam or write Odysseys, he will kindly pluck you a posy to still your sobs, and then let you go home.

"The design of God," says the great expounder, taking a fresh start from the skies, — "the design of God in creating woman was to complete man." "What is the chief end of man?" asks the Westminster Catechism. "Man's chief end is to glorify God and enjoy him forever." "What is the chief end of woman?"

"Woman's chief end is to complete man." True, just as much as God's design in creating man was to make a clay model for woman. "She has a mission, ... to be the mother and *the former of all the character of the human race.* For the first most important earthly period of life the race is committed to her,— for about twelve years almost entirely. The human family is what she makes them." Assertion may be met by assertion. The human race is committed to the father just as much as to the mother. The strongest force stamps character, whether it be that of father or mother. Often the good teachings of the mother are nullified by the bad example of the father. The child's mind and heart are the offspring of his father as well as of his mother. A mother cannot make the family happy or prosperous without the help, or in spite of the hindrance, of the father, any more than the father can without her or in spite of her. There is no such dividing line between father and mother. Their duty is inextricably interwoven. "She is the queen of the home, its centre, its light and glory." (Recent intelligence.) "Our mothers train us, and we owe everything to them. Our wives perfect all that is good in us, and no man is ashamed to say he is indebted to his wife for his happiness, his influence, and his character." Dr. Todd must be wary, or his felicity of style will get him into trouble. A double mortgage to the full extent on the same property renders a man liable to the law. If he owes everything to his mother, and yet is indebted to his wife for his happiness, his influence, and his character, we can only suggest to him the old Farmers' Almanac couplet, —

"Owen Moore has run away,
Owing more than he can pay."

"The home, the home, is the fountain of all that is good on earth." Are churches and Sunday schools and theological seminaries, then, fountains of unmixed evil? "Mother, wife, daughter, sister, are the tenderest, most endearing words in language. Woman is the highest, holiest, most precious gift to man." Does Dr. Todd intend this for argument? Does he mean that all homes are actually fountains of good; that all men pursue towards their mothers, wives, daughters, sisters, the tenderest and most endearing course of action; that all men recognize and treat the women with whom they come in contact as their highest, holiest, most precious gift, or that they come so near it as to make any change undesirable? If not, what does he mean? Why is he just now barking up that particular tree?

"If woman steps out of her sphere

and demands to be and to do what men do," — especially if she demands to be what men do, she is certainly an extraordinary woman, — "she will not be allowed to be a man, and be treated with the tenderness due to women." But if she stays a woman, will she be sure of that tenderness? "If she goes to Congress, she must also go to the heavy drudgery of earth," from which, as every one knows, she is now entirely exempt. Just here, in fact, Dr. Todd surpasses himself, and becomes continuously delightful. Whoever feels obliged to use his reason finds himself constantly hampered by its requirements, and can reach correct conclusions only by a slow, zigzag, and often perplexing path; but Dr. Todd is free from vexing limitations. His mind seems to be of that privileged sort that has no relation to facts. He assumes the point in question, he proves what was not denied, he disproves what was not asserted, he contradicts his own statements with a blithe unconsciousness truly refreshing. Indeed, his expertness in the latter feat is so great, that he may be said to have introduced a new form of proposition, the Kilkenny categorical; propositions which you have only to set side by side, and they immediately eat each other up. He labors under a chronic conviction that what women want is to be men. When they express a desire to be like men in respect to getting fair wages for work, he finds it a desire to wear — I borrow his own eloquence — pants. That is as near as he can get to the trouble of the time. He prepares an elaborate and formidable list of occupations, — trying up whales, cutting out tumors, stirring tan vats, bleeding calves, sticking swine, and many others equally æsthetic, — and felicitously adds, "Now she must go in for all this, if she leaves her sphere and tries to be a man." "Take off the robes, and put on pants, and show the limbs, and grace and mystery is" (a minor grammatical felicity) "all gone. And yet, to be like a man, you must doff your own dress and put on ours." "Dear sisters, you can't be good wives, mothers, and crowns of your families, and go into these things, — can you?"

Why not? Wives and mothers in their recognized "sphere" are called on to perform many services no more agreeable to woman's "refined," and far more exhaustive to her "delicate organization," than blacking boots. But why *must* the dear sisters go into all these things? Suppose they do want to be men, and suppose they succeed in becoming men, how does it follow that they are to be forced to "hang on the yard-arms"? Are men forced to hang on yard-arms? Does Dr. Todd earn his living by "burning over a smelting-furnace"? Has not a man, in spite of his right of suffrage, we will not say in consequence of it, power to say whether he will or will not spend his days as a barber? Do not men become doctors, lawyers, architects, artisans, laborers, as they will, guided by taste, fitness, or ambition? When women become men, why must they pass under a different law? Why must Lucretia Mott go to the Arctic Ocean and hunt seals, while Dr. Todd may stay at home and write sermons? Through stress of need, men sometimes pursue uncongenial occupations, but women do it already. By becoming men they would lose nothing in that direction. I know of no employment which men are absolutely forced to adopt, except that of war. If women vote, they must also "wear jack-boots and spurs." But is the wearing of jack-boots and spurs the only duty in war-time? During the late war was there not an army of women at home as large as the army of men in the field, and did they not work as long and as efficiently? And if war is so dear to the human heart that it cannot be relinquished, may not the regiments of women be detailed for services just as important as those of men, yet just as womanly as those of the host of women that were employed in our civil war? But is it an impossibility that men will by and by cease to let their angry passions rise to the point of tearing each other's eyes? Would it be an irreparable calamity, — would Dr. Todd, as a minister of the Gospel of Christ, consider it a consummation devoutly to be deprecated,—if the unfitness of jack-boots to woman should result, not in the discomfiture of woman, but in the abolition of jack-boots?

On the subject of voting, Dr. Todd comes out in force. "A great hue and cry is set up about the right of women to vote, and the cruelty of denying them this gift. Plainly this is merely a civil, and not a natural right. Minors, foreigners, and idiots are denied it." A mere bagatelle. What are the women fretting about? They are no worse off than idiots. Can any reasonable being be discontented who is allowed to exercise all the rights of infants in arms? "It would seem best .... for those who, at any hazard or labor, earn the property, to select the rulers." But there are thousands of women who earn property; therefore they shall *not* select rulers, according to Dr. Todd's logic. Man "wants rulers in reference to the industry and business of his age. Let him select them." Woman also wants rulers in reference to the business and industry of her age. Let her not select them. Dr. Todd says: "The wealth of the age is expended by woman, — earned by the man, — for the most part." As I write, I see load after load of salt hay going by from the marshes. The men who made that hay rose at one o'clock in the morning, rode two, three, or four miles to the marsh, and worked till night in cutting and curing it. But the women who stayed at home rose at the same hour, prepared the men's breakfast, packed their dinner and lunch, and, in cooking, cleaning, making, and mending, worked just as long and just as hard as the men. The money for that hay will not be paid into their hands, but they earned it just as much as the men. Dr. Todd avows that men are indebted to their wives for their influence and character. But it is influence and character that determine income. "Being a widow or fatherless, is a misfortune." (Not always.) "But the husband or father earned the property, and voted as long as he lived. It may be a misfortune that the property does not now vote, but not so great a misfortune to the world as to have the sex go out of their sphere and enter into political life." The disputed point is, whether voting is woman's sphere. You shall not vote, says Dr. Todd, because it is going out of your sphere! And this is the good, strong common-sense which is to commend itself to the great majority of American women!

"Moreover, there is something so unseemly in having women wading in the dirty waters of politics, draggling and wrangling round the ballot-boxes, e. g. mingling with the mobs and rowdies in New York City, that I wonder she ever thinks of it." Doubtless she never would have thought of it, had she dreamed that it would excite Dr. Todd's wonder; but as the deed is already done, perhaps the next best thing is to inquire who made the political waters dirty. Who is it that is draggling and wrangling around the ballot-boxes? Must we say men? But woman is man's highest, holiest, most precious gift. It is to these draggling, wrangling mobs and rowdies that this holy gift is intrusted. A man who has kept his gift sacred at home for three hundred and sixty-four days of the year will not be likely to desecrate it at the polls on the three hundred and sixty-fifth. And if men are so bad that they cannot be trusted to vote with women, is it beyond question that they ought to be trusted to vote for women?

Again, suppose the ballot to be extended to American women, how many of them will mingle with the mobs and rowdies of New York City? How many of the women in Dr. Todd's congregation will take the first train for New York on election day? And even in New York, who are the women that will draggle and wrangle around the ballot-boxes? Is it the women of Grace Church and Trinity, of Dr. Thompson's and Dr. Chapin's and Dr. Adams's churches? Do Dr. Thompson, Dr. Chapin, and Dr. Todd draggle and wrangle around the ballot-boxes? and are their wives any more likely to do it than themselves? We will not of course hazard the conjecture that the female mind might invent a separate arrangement for taking the female vote; but draggling and wrangling do not seem to be the necessary concomitants of voting among men. And if a man feels that his wife's character is not strong enough to enable her to deposit a ballot once a year without demoralizing herself and disgracing him, he can fall back to the old English common law, and shut her up at home till election is over. So any woman who feels within herself that her womanliness would be injured by going to the polls, that her dignity cannot stand so trying a process, has always the simple remedy of staying away. Let no woman be led into temptation. But to keep all the dear sisters from the polls because a few of them are too weak to be trusted there, is purchasing peace at a great cost. That the advocates of voting are "moral Camillas, who clamor and disgust their sex and ours," is nothing to the purpose, unless unattractive manners are recognized as a disqualification for the exercise of the right of suffrage. Unless it is demanded that a man shall be agreeable before he is allowed to vote, there is no justice in demanding that a woman shall be agreeable.

The complicated question of wages has no complications for Dr. Todd. Minds of the best endowments and the highest culture have given their energies to this subject, yet have failed to lead the world to a satisfactory conclusion. Dr. Todd takes hold of it, and difficulties disappear like flax in the fire. He confesses that it is a hard problem to solve, and immediately goes and solves it. How, will any one guess? By saying, first, we can't have justice in these matters; and secondly, we already have it! "We can't have justice in these matters. But bear in mind, that God has put the labor and the duty on men to support the families; . . . . and to do it, and bear the responsibility, he must receive wages accordingly. Is it, then, so very unjust that woman, who has no such responsibility, does not receive so high wages?"

Here, straightening out the tangle of talk, we find three distinct lines of response to the complaint of low wages:—

First, We can't have justice in these matters, illustrated by the case of an excellent pastor who receives only four hundred dollars salary, and of many who receive five or six hundred dollars.

Second, We have justice, for men have the responsibility, and therefore they ought to have the wages.

Third, The great laws of political economy, especially the law of supply and demand, are beyond reach of human law and power, therefore all talk is useless.

To the first we may say that the impossibility of securing justice does not stop the mouths of the excellent pastors any more than those of women. Every reader of religious newspapers knows that the cry of the clergy for larger salaries is an exceeding great and bitter cry. But I think there is no record of any attempt by Dr. Todd to hush them by telling them that they can't have justice, — that their demand is vain so long as there are thousands ready to underbid them, *and* do the work cheaper, — that the demand will pay in proportion to the supply, and no human power can alter this. Yet it is difficult to see why the suggestions which are thought so salutary and sufficient in the one case are not equally so in the other.

For the second. Does responsibility indeed enter into the calculation of wages? Does a mechanic with six children receive more money for his work than a mechanic with no children? Then it would seem that Dr. Todd's third proposition cannot be true, at least not in the common acceptation of its terms.

Demand pays in proportion to the supply of responsibility, not solely to the supply of work. But why then is not woman's responsibility also taken into the account. Why do not school committees pay to female teachers who have families to support the same salary which they pay to male teachers similarly situated? Dr. Todd indeed denies that there is any female responsibility. The woman on whom his eye is chronically set "has no such responsibility." The world, as Dr. Todd sees it, is evidently modelled on the heaven which one of our exquisite little Sunday-school songs so poetically portrays: —

"No wickedness there, not a shade of transgression,
Nor poverty there, — no, the saints are all wealthy, —
Nor sickness can reach them, — that country is healthy."

In his apocalyptic vision he sees women as queens, walking gracefully in waving robes, hearing only the most endearing words, receiving only such careful and gentle treatment as their refined organization requires, yet fired with an unaccountable desire to leave it all and rush to the slaughter-house to knock down oxen on their own account, and receive as much money for it, to spend on rings, as men receive to buy bread and butter for the whole family. He does not recognize — he at least makes no provision for — the thousands of women who have their own bread to earn, and often that of relatives. "The wolf is at the door," cry these women. "We are starving in the house. Untie our hands that we may have a fairer chance at the foe!" "The house, the house," cries Dr. Todd, "is the place for women. Wolf-fighting belongs to men. Woman's delicate organization cannot endure so long as his," — and goes back into his study.

For the third proposition. If it be

true, why does he make the first and second? Because he is gifted with a brilliant inability to distinguish between what is true and what is untrue, what is pertinent and what is impertinent. To him a principle, a fact, an obligation, an incident, a possibility, all belong to one class. He tosses together a heap of bricks and stones and mortar and rubbish, with a granite block or two, and thinks it is a marble monument. And men upturn to it solemn, admiring eyes, and commend it to American women!

But Dr. Todd does recognize the fact that "there are over seventy thousand more females" (what felicity should we have missed had he called these females women!) "in Massachusetts than there are men, and probably twice this number in the State of New York. . . . . Our young men go off early in life, leaving homes, mothers, and sisters behind them. . . . .

Now the question comes, what shall be done in behalf of these thousands of virtuous, educated, and noble girls?" At last, then, we have got Dr. Todd face to face, not with a phantom of his own brain, but with a real difficulty. How does he meet it?

"The cry is, 'Make them into clerks, book-keepers, bankers, and give them all the employments of men.' . . . . Let us think it over a moment. We are sorry for this state of things and wish we could remedy it." That is hopeful; Dr. Todd might have put his hands into his pockets, and said he was glad of it! But what is he sorry for?—that the seventy thousand girls are born, or that the seventy thousand young men went West? Would he think it better for themselves and society that they should have stayed at home? "But suppose now we make these girls into clerks, in stores, in the counting-room, in the insurance-office, in the bank, — say ten thousand in Massachusetts and twenty thousand in New York, — don't we displace just so many young men, drive them off to the West, prevent so many new families from being established here, take away thirty thousand chances of marriage from these females, and enhance the evil we are trying to remedy? Is it a blessing to woman to lessen her opportunities for marriage? This state of things will eventually right itself, but it bears hard upon women now; but to displace men, to increase the evil, to plan for a present exigency by upturning all the arrangements of Providence, is not wise. We must look at the grand total of result. It is *not* that we wish to keep women from enjoying anything and everything that is for the best good of her sex. I speak of displacing men, and forcing them away. I might add, that, from the very instincts of the human heart, every public employment diminishes woman's chance of marriage, and in proportion to its publicity."

So then it seems that, if women leave their sphere, they must go into ore-digging and hod-carrying, timber-cutting and log-driving, but they may not go into banks and insurance-offices. There is no objection to displacing young men from yard-arms, but they must not be displaced from the counting-room. The law of supply and demand must regulate wages, but it cannot be trusted to regulate work. Employers may justly pay women starvation prices, but women must not seek any other than the starvation places. No moral sense need keep a tailor from oppressing his needle-women, but moral considerations must keep needle-women from taking refuge in a strawberry-garden. No girl must enter a shop or a school-room, — Dr. Todd does not say school-room, but he must mean it, since a school-room is a more public place than an insurance-office, and a woman there displaces a man just as certainly, — no girl must enter a shop or a school-room, because she displaces a man and diminishes her chance of marriage. Dr. Todd elsewhere tells us that he has been for forty years connected with female seminaries. Female seminaries are chiefly under the charge of female principals and teachers. Has he taken care to inform those teachers that they are upturning the arrangements of Providence? Has he exhorted them in season and out of season, for as long a time as the Israelites were wandering in the wilderness, to leave their schools and go home, that they might be ready in case a suitor should happen along?

What does Dr. Todd propose? He shuts the avenues to employment: what does he open instead?

Nothing. Absolutely nothing.

He has no more to say on the subject. He takes up at once another theme. The seventy thousand women may sit on the curb-stone and suck their thumbs, for anything he has to suggest. It bears rather hard on woman now, he admits, but it will eventually right itself. Sucking your thumb is not a lucrative, nor, after a certain age, an honorable or agreeable occupation, but in course of seventy or a thousand years something better may offer; which is consoling. Starving is not pleasant now; but to stave off starvation by going into a dry-goods shop and upturning all the arrangements of Providence is not wise. A pretty Providence, truly, that scatters through the State seventy thousand more women than can be married, and then forbids them to do anything else than marry! A Providence after Dr. Todd's own heart, that tosses together a mass of incongruities and calls it an arrangement! — an arrangement so stable and efficient that a girl can upset it with a yardstick!

And this is what our religious teachers call felicity of thought, and our secular teachers, good, strong common-sense.

Dr. Todd next settles the question of female education and female colleges. "If it ministers to variety to call a girls' school a college, it is very harmless." He is willing the fair ones should amuse themselves with edge-tools to that extent. But open the knife? No, no, pet, it will cut its little hands! "As for training young ladies through a long intellectual course, as we do young men, it can never be done, they will die in the process. Give woman all the advantages and all the education which her organization, so tender and delicate, will bear, but don't try to make the anemone into an oak," and so forth. Thus the tender and delicate organization stands in the way, not only of Herschels and Laplaces, but of ordinary college graduates. Doubtless our colleges are in many respects excellent institutions, but I have never been so impressed with the weight of learning invariably brought from them as to feel that the female brain would hopelessly stagger under it. However, Dr. Todd says it would, and it is perhaps unseemly to discuss the question. But he is willing to declare "deliberately that the female has mind enough, talent enough, to go through a complete college course, but her physical organization will never admit of it, as a general thing.

I think the great danger of our day is forcing the intellect of woman beyond what her physical organization will possibly bear. We want to put our daughters at school at six, and have their education completed at eighteen. A girl would feel mortified not to be through schooling by the time she reaches that age" (a statement that will surprise girls, I think). "In these years the poor thing has her brain crowded with history, grammar, arithmetic, geography, natural history, chemistry, physiology, botany, astronomy, rhetoric, natural and moral philosophy, metaphysics, French, often German, Latin, perhaps Greek, reading, spelling, committing poetry, writing compositions, drawing, painting, &c., &c., *ad infinitum.* Then, out of school hours, from three to six hours of severe toil at the piano. She must be on the strain all the school hours, study in the evening till her eyes ache, her brain whirls, her spine yields and gives way, and she comes through the process of education, enervated, feeble, without courage or vigor, elasticity or strength. Alas! must we crowd education upon our daughters, and, for the sake of having them 'intellectual,' make them puny, nervous, and their whole earthly existence a struggle between life and death?"

But Dr. Todd wanders from his point. In fact, it is always hazardous to predict from the beginning of his sentences what the end will be. He starts with a disclaimer against female colleges; but here we find ourselves in the midst of a protest against female seminaries. So it is not simply that girls are unable to go through the course prescribed for boys; they are also unequal to that prescribed for girls. The reason alleged is, that their health will not permit it. "Now that we have taken woman in hand, we are in danger of educating her into the grave, taking her out of her own beautiful, honored sphere, and making her an hermaphrodite, instead of what God made her to be."

Why, here is still another fresh charge under cover of the old one, — a wheel within the wheel within the first wheel. Is Dr. Todd springing a trap upon us? All through his discussion of the subject, he has been deprecating female education solely on the ground of female weakness; but in the very last sentence he brings up quietly, as if it were one and the same thing, an entirely new and distinct objection, — strong-mindedness. Is this fair? His woman being educated into the grave, the natural inference is that she will stay there;

but before the breath is fairly out of her body, presto! she is up again and whirling out of her sphere! Now, with all deference to Dr. Todd's masculine strength, and to that long and severe course of intellectual training which it has enabled him to undergo, and which has so well fitted him for his sphere, we must submit that this is putting rather too fine a point upon it. We may educate our girls to death, or we may educate them into woman's-rights women, but we cannot do both. Perhaps a woman may as well be dead as be voting, but they are not yet synonymous terms. A girl cannot be in her grave and be going around lecturing at the same time. Dr. Todd may have his choice of the two evils. Which does he mean, then,—that girls cannot be educated as men are, because they will die in the process, or because they will mount his pet bugbear, ride away from their spheres, and try to be men?

If any other Providence than Dr. Todd's were concerned, one might be disposed to inquire its object in giving woman more mind than she can cultivate. "A little farm well tilled" is supposed to be more profitable than ever so great a reach of waste land. Why endow woman with as much mind as man, if she is forever incapacitated from training it? But Dr. Todd's Providence is *sui generis*, and we will simply meet his assertion with another, — that the female not only has mind enough, talent enough, but also body enough, to go through a complete college course. Dr. Todd judges, from what he has seen in female schools, that it cannot be done. I judge, from what I have seen in and out of female schools, that it can be done. He laments that, between the ages of six and eighteen, the poor thing has her brain crowded with history, grammar, and the rest. I affirm that if, between the ages of six and eighteen, a girl cannot get all those things into her brain without crowding it, she *is* a poor thing. A girl can go to school, pursue all the studies which Dr. Todd enumerates, except *ad infinitum*, know them,— not as well as a chemist knows chemistry, or a botanist botany, but as well as they are known by boys of her age and training, as well indeed as they are known by many college-taught men, enough at least to be a solace and resource to her, — then graduate before she is eighteen, and come out of school as healthy, as fresh, as eager as she went in, and never through her subsequent life know a week's, scarcely a day's illness. I know this, for I have seen it. Nature harmonizes body and mind in woman as well as in man. Aching eyes and whirling brain and yielding spine need no more attend intellectual activity in girls than in boys. Let a girl have a strong constitution, a vigorous body, and a sound mind, to begin with, — let her be taught to work, to play, to study, and not to dawdle, — let her have plenty of fresh air, wholesome food, early sleep, active out-door exercise, and healthful dress, all of which are compatible with a long intellectual course, — and she need fear nothing that seminaries or colleges have to offer. The reason why girls in school and out of school are puny, enervated, and exhausted is not that they are girls, but that they have inherited feeble constitutions, or they have been injured by improper food, improper dress, late hours, unnatural and unwholesome excitement, or they have been committed to unskilful and incompetent teachers; and among incompetent teachers I should certainly reckon those of Dr. Todd's acquaintance,—teachers who, besides the routine of school, require from three to six hours of severe daily toil on the piano. I do not know any such teachers. I never heard of any such practice. In all the female schools I ever knew, music was considered as a study, and was included in the regular course. It certainly does not demand such a lion's share of time in boys' schools or colleges, and therefore, in considering a girl's chances of passing through a college safely, these three or six hours may be counted in her favor.

A newspaper paragraph circulating while I am writing is so apposite that I cannot refrain from transcribing it.

The London correspondent of the "Tribune" calls attention to a work little known even in England, — "Notes of a Twelve Years' Voyage of Discovery in the First Six Books of the Æneis," by Dr. James Henry. The author's ability as a commentator has been acknowledged by Mr. Conington, who has profited by it in his recent translation of the same epic. But the most remarkable feature of this persistent study is thus stated by Dr. Henry himself: —

"I have been, as the title imports, twelve years, twelve of the fairest years of my life, engaged in this work; encouraged by no one, approved by no one, patronized by no one, receiving no particle of assistance either at home or abroad from any one of all the numerous persons who have, with more or less success, cultivated the same author, except alone the assistance which I have reared and created for myself in my own daughter, who has already, at the age of twenty-two, arrived at such a degree of knowledge of the subject, that I have not printed a single comment without first submitting it to her censorship. Many and valuable have been the suggestions I have received from her, although I have not specially stated the fact, except at Æn. II. 683," in the note on which he remarks: "I cannot refuse myself the pleasure of informing my readers that the above very new, and, it seems to me, very true explanation of this difficult passage was suggested to me by one whose zealous assistance and co-operation has all along not only lightened but rendered delightful to me the otherwise almost intolerable labor of this work, — I mean my beloved daughter, Katharine Olivia Henry."

Study is healthful. Real study conduces to peace of mind and body.

Many girls, and boys too, are incapable of it. I have known parents lament the effects of hard study on their children, when those children never knew an hour's hard study, and never could compass it if their life depended on it. What they suffer from is inability to study, not study. Parental ignorance, vice, weakness, or mismanagement has given them bodies and souls alike nerveless and flaccid. They can go to parties, follow the fashions, lounge over books, perhaps pore and worry over them; but they are utterly incapable of concentration, energy, struggle, victory. Their minds are inane and their bodies drooping. Others have fine physical powers in which their puny souls are wellnigh lost. Others have strong souls, but chained to a body of death. By all means let such children quietly fall out of the ranks. It is only adding cruelty to cruelty to require of them what can be done only by able-bodied souls and able-souled bodies; but to make them the standard — to force healthy, jubilant beings, all thrilling and tingling with life, to keep step with them — is a device worthy of Dr. Todd. If, instead of laboring to dwarf woman's intellect to the measure of her crippled physical powers, he had labored to raise her physical powers to the height of her uncrippled intellect, — if, instead of showing parents that they wrong their children by trying to educate them, he had shown the earlier and deeper wrong of multiplying children too feeble to be educated, — he would, I was about to say, have labored to some purpose; but remembering the manner in which he espouses a cause, I withdraw the suggestion, and only beg him to fight it out on the line which he has already taken. The discovery of the laws of life is difficult and delicate. To put Dr. Todd on the scent might be fatal to the search. Fortunately for mankind he is committed against its improvement. So far from endeavoring to ascertain the conditions of advance, he strenuously preaches that the true mission and highest glory of the languid, enervated, and puny beings whom he portrays is to reproduce themselves in the greatest possible numbers.

His conclusion of the whole matter is, that "the root of the great error of our day is, that *woman is to be made independent and self-supporting,* — precisely what she never can be, because God never designed she should be. Her support, her dignity, her beauty, her honor and happiness, lie in her dependence as wife, mother, and daughter. Any other theory is rebellion against

God's law of the sexes, — against marriage," and so forth.

"O woman! your worst enemy is he who scouts at marriage, ... who would cruelly lift you out of your sphere and try to reverse the very laws of God; who tries to make you believe that you will find independence, wealth, and renown in man's sphere, when your only safety and happiness is in patiently, lovingly, and faithfully performing the duties and enacting the relations of your own sphere. Women of my country! beloved in your own sphere, can't you see that man, rough, stern, ... head, ... woman, ... patient, ... loving, ... heart." I give only the catch-words; every one can fill the gaps for himself.

It is the old refrain. Everything is just as it should be, except that women are not contented. They are beloved and honored in their own sphere. Why do they try to leave it? Women who have been oppressed and neglected by their natural protectors among men, or who have lost them through illness or death, claim opportunity to protect themselves, and are met by the cry, "The great error of our day is that woman is to be made self-supporting." Forced to do man's work, woman asks as far as possible man's advantages, and is told that God never designed she should support herself. Seventy thousand women, for whom no man has been or can be provided, are told that their support, their dignity, their beauty and honor and happiness, lie in dependence on some man. Any other theory is rebellion against God's law of the sexes, and of the universe generally.

Dr. Todd's aim, so far as he has any, seems to be at unmarried women, especially in the latter part of his essay. But if he will examine the reports and records of the Woman's Rights conventions, I think he will find "Mrs." quite as often as "Miss" against the names. If he will investigate the alleged grievances of women, I think he will find the complaint of wives quite as long and loud and bitter as that of maidens. If any women scout at marriage, it is as often they who have tried it as they who have not. But taking him on his own ground, what would he have these unmarried women do? What course does he propose to the girls who have left school and are entering their womanhood? Marriage, marriage, marriage, is the one profession, the one sphere, the one blessing which he holds out to them, —

> "A sovereign balm for every wound,
> A cordial for their fears."

He sees honor, dignity, support, nowhere else. To this, and this alone, he urges them by every consideration earthly and heavenly. What then? Shall the girls take matters into their own hands? Shall they swarm into the counting-rooms, the factories, the colleges, the theological seminaries, drop a courtesy to the young men, and say, "Sir, will you please to marry me?" As for sitting at home and waiting for the young men to come to them, they do that now. Unless Dr. Todd means that they are to go out into the highways and hedges and compel men to come in, it is difficult to see what he does mean. If he permitted himself to use his eyes, — a habit which he gives no sign of ever having fallen into, — he would see that reluctance to marriage is not the great or the growing fault of women. He would see with deep inward shame not unmixed with pity, that mental idleness, lack of purpose and interest in life, poverty, weakness, and bad teachings, have made women so ready to accept any sort of marriage, that too often the womanly name is lightly spoken, the womanly assent lightly valued. That which should be to men the prize of life they count but an ordinary commodity. Wives are to be selected, not won. Love is a serving-man, not a conqueror. Marriage is a provision; an occupation, an arrangement, any coarse and common thing, and Dr. Todd will have it so.

And the religious newspapers and the secular newspapers join voices and shout Amen!

Here Dr. Todd's argument ends, but his peroration is so characteristic that one cannot refrain from a few notes of admiration. "I have spoken to you, gentle ones, kindly and faithfully." This is a continuation of the conciliatory style, and is always to be adopted in addressing women. "Very likely I may have a torrent of abuse poured upon me for it; but it is time that your real friends should no longer have utterance choked." Utterance choked! Have such real friends as Dr. Todd had their utterance choked? Then surely they can talk as well without their throats as with them, for his talk has been talked from the foundation of the world, — at least as far back towards it as this generation can remember. He might have listened any time within the last ten years, and found men still harping on my daughter on precisely his own key, though it must be admitted that the peculiar felicity of Dr. Todd's expression gives to the antiquity of his thought a piquancy truly original. "I have tried to select smooth stones from the brook for my sling, and not to wound those whom I would defend." Is this, then, the way to defend women, by slinging stones at them? And does it mend the matter to say that he did not mean to hurt them? Would he fire a broadside into a female seminary, and excuse himself to the bleeding, moaning victims on the plea that he took round shot and not conical? "And having said this, I only add, that no provocation will force me to speak on this subject again."

Ungentle ones, we fear, will add that nothing in his essay becomes him like the ending of it.

And all the Wackford Squeerses who have gone into the business of newspaper editing smack their lips over this twopenn'orth of milk in a mug of lukewarm water, and cry out to their unlucky readers, "Here 's richness!"

Proving Dr. Todd wrong is, I am quite aware, a totally different thing from proving any one else right. The fitness of female suffrage does not depend upon the character of its adherents or opponents. The question stands precisely where it stood before Dr. Todd took up his pen. It has been so long discussed, with so much ability and so much disability, that it would seem as if every wise and every foolish thing that could be said about it had been already said, and one feels disposed to apologize at every step for reopening the subject. But the publication of Dr. Todd's essay, and its reception by our reverend assemblies of divines and our social philosophers, speedily transform the amiable disposition into an impulse to follow the example of the renowned Jenny Geddes, and fling a stool at their heads. A generation that accepts "Woman's Rights" need not complain of anything that may be offered it in the way of triteness.

A remarkable feature of the discussion is the scarcity of reasons brought against female suffrage. There seems to be a sort of instinct against it, but scarcely anything that can be called a reason. This instinct may in itself be the best of reasons, and if opponents would only plant themselves there, simply affirming,

"I do not like you, Dr. Fell,
The reason why I cannot tell,
But this alone I know full well,
I do not like you, Dr. Fell,"

they would hold a strong position. But the things brought forward as arguments are so flimsy, that argument and instinct are blown away together.

Nor is the spirit in which the question is discussed always unexceptionable. There is something like taunt on the woman side, and something like threat on the man side, not unnatural in the circumstances, but both alike unworthy of the cause and unfruitful of good. Female suffrage is not an affair of antagonism between man and woman. It is not a struggle in which women are to be the gainers and men the losers. It is one in which both are to gain or both to lose alike. If women ought to vote, a woman's vote is as much a man's right as it is a woman's right. If women ought not to vote, a woman's vote is as great an impertinence to a woman as to a man. It is not even whether women wish to vote: it is whether they have a right to vote; whether they ought to vote; whether the country needs the votes of her women, and can afford to do without them.

I believe it is seldom, if ever, denied that women have abstractly an equal right with men to vote. The objection is, that the exercise of that right will change, first, the womanly nature, and second, the womanly sphere. It will make women bold, pushing, masculine. It is essentially unwomanly.

But what is it that is unwomanly, — the possession of political opinion, or the expression of that opinion by walking to the vestry, or the town-house, or the public hall, and putting a piece of paper in a box? Not surely the former. Surely we all know that women are already in the habit of forming opinions on politics. More than this, their interest in and their knowledge of politics are exactly in proportion to their intelligence, to their intellect; not at all in proportion to their amiability or their femininity. A woman may be ignorant of politics, and be graceful, lovely, fascinating, or she may be coarse, harsh, unattractive; but I venture to say there is not in the country a woman of active intelligence who is not conversant with the general state and aims of political parties. Some of the women whose names have a political prominence are among the most attractive women of their time, others are among the most repulsive. So it seems that the holding of political opinion does not of itself change character. And if a woman is not demoralized by saying to her husband and her visitors that she considers Mr. A. Johnson an able and admirable President, would she be demoralized by dropping into a box a vote to that effect?

So when it is said that voting is out of the womanly sphere, will any one be so good as to tell us what it is that is out of her sphere, the possession or the expression of political opinion? But possession, as we have seen, she already holds. Wives, mothers, daughters, who discharge with fidelity every domestic and social duty, are conversant with national and international affairs. Nay, I have no hesitation in affirming that exactly in proportion as a woman is clear-sighted, far-sighted, judicious in her domestic and social administration, in just that proportion is her judgment of public affairs clear and just and wise. Faithful in least, faithful in much, is not the axiom of religion only. Stories, theories, rumors, assert the contrary; appearances sometimes indicate the contrary, but I never knew a fact that did not confirm this statement.

Is it then the act of casting a ballot which is to draw or drive woman out of her sphere, — this woman who in the centre of her sphere has already performed all the work preliminary to voting, whose opinions are matured, whose decisions formed? But on occasion of a concert, a lecture, even a political address, she already goes to the same place and sees very nearly the same men that she would on election-days. At what moment then, at what point, does she take the fatal step that puts her beyond her sphere?

Is it that the interest in and knowledge of politics requisite for voting will take too much time that ought to be devoted to other and nearer duties by the ordinary woman? But what proportion of the time of ordinary men — merchants, mechanics, laborers — is spent in politics? For how many hours in the day, for how many days in the year, for how many weeks in their lives, are they drawn away from their counting-rooms and workshops by political exigencies? Do they not acquire their opinions unconsciously as a part of their recreation, and is not the time spent in voting so small as to exercise no appreciable influence on the ordinary year's wages of the common workingman? Does the wife of the butcher or of the shoemaker suffer any measurable deprivation from her husband's absorption in politics? Is there anything in the nature of woman which would lead us to suppose that her devotion to politics would be greater than that of her husband or that to her husband? or that it would be more difficult for her to acquire knowledge than for him? On the contrary, would not the change from the narrow circle of her domestic home to the great circle of her national home be a benefit to her? Would it not be to her as to her husband, and even more than to her husband, inasmuch as the change to her would be greater, a refreshment rather than an additional task? Would it not give a spring to her mind, a quickening to her life, that would react favorably on her home? Would not the very act of gaining political knowledge fit her the better for administering her domestic government?

Is it that voting, though an innocent thing enough of itself, is the forerunner of many evils, is but the opening to woman of offices and employments that have hitherto belonged and are suitable only to man? that female suffrage means female electioneering, stump-speaking, office-holding, and other ills equally unpleasant to contemplate?

But suppose the right of ballot should indeed fashion womankind politically after the similitude of mankind, how extensive would be the evil deprecated? There is indeed among men much political wire-pulling, yet how few, in proportion to the rest of mankind, are the political wire-pullers! Members of Congress are many, but they do not show up largely among our neighbors. The name of political office-holders is Legion, yet somehow they seldom drop in to tea. And of those that do hold office, how many hold it in the most imperceptible manner! You may be for weeks in the company of a modest selectman, town-clerk, churchwarden, and never discover the fact,—may imagine all the while that he is only a lawyer or a grocer. If then the holding of office interferes so little with men's business, why should it any more interfere with women's? If so few farmers are called from their farms, and shoemakers from their benches, what reason have we for supposing that more cooks will be drawn from their ranges or washerwomen from their tubs? Moreover, there are thousands more of women than of men, at least in Massachusetts; and if from Massachusetts men can be spared and not missed, how much more the women! At present, when a man is elected to an office incompatible with and less important than his regular business, he simply declines it. Women can always do the same. No one proposes to force them to be Presidents or even town treasurers.

But we need not go so far as this, for Nature anticipates us. These things, we say, are all unnatural, and therefore they are objectionable. They are unwomanly. But if they are unwomanly, women as a class will never take to them. If home-life is the natural sphere of woman, nothing but necessity will ever drive her from it. Certainly no allurements will ever draw her out. We are never allured to that for which we have no natural taste. Nothing is safer to trust in, nothing is harder to force, than nature. If women have a natural distaste and unfitness for public life, there is no more danger of their voting themselves into public officers than there is of men's voting themselves into nursery-maids. Undoubtedly there are women — exceptional cases, if you please — who are much better fitted to hold office than most men. There are women who are better orators, better mathematicians, better business managers than most men. Voting will not make them so, as absence of voting has not prevented their becoming such. These women may possibly become public officers, but such women always have become public officers. Fitness for the work was long ago considered a vindication of the work. There is no record that the most conservative Israelites ever objected to Deborah's judgeship, or that Hilkiah the priest, or Shaphan the scribe, or Asahiah the king's servant, had any misgiving about going to the college to consult Huldah the prophetess who dwelt in it, or that the Republican party ever rejected the votes which Miss Dickinson's eloquence brought out in the campaign of 1860. If the right of suffrage shall result in bringing woman from the domestic hearth to the public hall, it will only show that we have all been wrong together in restricting her to the former. Certainly we shall never know what woman's natural sphere is till she has an absolutely unrestricted power of choice,—that is, until her nature is suffered to have free play.

Do women indeed not wish to vote? That is the best of reasons why they should not be forced to vote, but no reason at all why they should not be allowed and required to vote. Those of us who are Orthodox Congregationalists know very well that we never excuse our fellow-sinners from repentance because they do not wish to repent. This very fact of unwillingness we bring as the heaviest charge against them, and with all the more vehemence urge them to a change of heart as the necessary precursor of a change of life. If women ought to vote, their indifference to voting is but a sign that they are dead in trespasses and sins.

Moreover, it cannot be denied that there are many women who do wish to vote. On what ground shall they be debarred from doing so? Even though it were granted — what is by no means proved — that the majority of American women do not wish to vote, how does that affect the minority who do wish it? Because A, B, and C do not wish to exercise a certain right, shall D not be allowed to exercise it?

Or is it that women are, by nature, education, or both, unfit to exercise the right of suffrage? This, if true, is pertinent and conclusive. I am not prepared to say that it is not true. Undoubtedly a very large number of women are by their education unfit to vote; but does the same standard of fitness apply to men? Are American women, as a class, more unfit to vote than Irishmen? Are they less capable of understanding issues involved, and of passing judgment upon measures proposed, than negroes who have been slaves for generations? And if their minds are so narrow that they cannot comprehend, and so feeble that they cannot entertain, national questions, — if they are so unable to control their impulses and conquer their prejudices that they cannot act wisely in national contingencies, — are they fit to be the wives and mothers, the companions and teachers, of those on whom thought and action devolve?

But whatever may be true of the masses of women, it will not be denied that there are individual women, and a good many of them, who are more fit to vote than the majority of voters. It will not be denied that the Mrs. Stowes, the Miss Mitchells, the Mary Lyons, the Mrs. Mills, the Madame de Staëls, are as able to form an intelligent opinion, even upon questions of finance and internal improvements, as the laborers who are digging in the canals, and the shoemakers pegging on their benches. If fitness is the standard, why is fitness excluded from, and unfitness admitted to, the polls?

Does the allegation of female unfitness come with a good grace from the lips of men? The suffrage has hitherto been in their hands; what is the result? Politics, which, whether considered as a science or an art, is one of the most noble and dignified subjects that can occupy the human mind, has fallen to the level of a miserable scramble for place and pelf. Men have made it so foul and degraded a thing that its very touch is thought to be contamination to women, and the name of politician is a reproach. The polls, under the exclusive control of men, have become a place of such desperate resort that the word is a proverb for vileness and violence. The houses of Congress are composed of men, theoretically of the ablest men in the nation; and in perhaps the greatest emergency of modern times they only succeeded in making a patchwork of reconstruction, which the President thrusts his fingers through the moment they are gone home; and if, alarmed, they rush back and patch up the ghastly rent, no sooner is quiet restored, and Congress dispersed, than the restless Presidential fingers are poking through another thin place. It is not a question of wise politics, but of skilful workmanship. We need not inquire whether they are masters of statecraft; they are not even mechanics. Legislation is in the hands of men, and they cross and recross the great currents of society as unconsciously and as placidly as if those currents had no existence; they tinker at the great natural laws of trade as confidently as they hammer the red-hot iron upon their own anvils; they tamper with the great natural laws of morals and manners as boldly as if history had left no record of previous similar attempts, and the kingdom of Heaven were to be taken by an order of the General Court. All official appointments are in the hands of men, and they have made Fernando Wood Mayor of New

York, and sent John Morissey to Congress, and put Andrew Johnson in the Presidential chair.

One kind of unfitness in women is said to be their intense personality. They never consider a subject fairly. They always look at every question with reference to some man. In the light of recent events, this tendency seems anything but an unfitness. If the party of freedom and progress had looked a little more closely at the men whom they set up for leaders, it would have been better for the party and better for the country.

But cannot men be trusted with the interests of their own wives, mothers, daughters, sisters? Certainly they cannot. Men are in the constant daily habit of doing injustice to wife, mother, daughter, sister. The minds of women are dwarfed, their health ruined, their fortunes squandered, their hearts broken, by men who stand to them in the nearest and dearest relations. Do not men themselves see this? Do men trust men,—even their own fathers, brothers, and sons? Do not the men who ask this question know scores of men to whom they would be unwilling to trust the interests of their own mothers and sisters and daughters? Moreover, there are many women who have none of these relationships to flee to, who stand alone. If society were millennial, if men and women were infallible, if every woman on arriving at maturity became the justly beloved and honored wife of a justly beloved and honored husband, and remained so during all the years of their lives, she might safely trust her interests in his hands; but with a society so far deflected from uprightness as ours, with human life so far from its ideal, there is no class that can safely delegate its interests to another class. It is because human nature is defective that human laws are made; and human nature being defective, it is never safe to trust it with irresponsible power.

But will the incursion of woman upon the ballot-box seriously mend matters? I fear not. Accomplished in the manner and to the extent proposed, I honestly think not. The association of man and woman is natural. Their dissociation in politics is unnatural. The exclusion of any one class from an equal position with another class regarding affairs in which both have an equal interest, and to which both contribute an equal support, is arbitrary and unnatural, and all things unnatural are wrong and hurtful. On this ground female suffrage seems to me a right and wise measure, and its prohibition an absurdity. But beyond this all is fog. What definite benefit is to accrue to woman or to the State from indiscriminate female suffrage, I must confess, after all the talk, I fail to see. The volume of the vote will be increased, but I do not see that its proportion will be affected; and the proportion of the vote and not its volume is the quarter from which danger threatens. True, in a republican government, the broader the basis, the better, provided it be sound; but if it be not sound, how can its breadth be an element of strength? Believing, as I do, most firmly, that the right of suffrage belongs to woman in precisely the same measure as to man,—no more and no less,—and that it will do for woman precisely what it does for man,—no better and no worse,—still, were the alternative presented to me of changing the basis of suffrage, either by extending the franchise indiscriminately to women, or by still further restricting it among men, I think I should unhesitatingly choose the latter. I would far sooner trust the welfare of the country to the freely acting wisdom of intelligent and virtuous men, than to the wisdom of intelligent and virtuous men and women, hampered, baffled, and overborne by the folly of unintelligent and vicious men and women. On matters of so grave and vast importance, subjects which have received the profound attention of the deepest thinkers, it may seem presumptuous for a "commoner" to advance an opinion. But it is to the glory of the thinkers that they have reasoned so closely, and spoken so clearly, as to have brought the subject within the scope of common minds, and every day brings us visibly nearer and nearer to the time when the commonest minds will be called on to pass judgment, which, if not absolutely final, will be relatively so to many, and of the most serious moment to all.

To many the flimsiness and folly of the arguments brought against female suffrage have been its strongest recommendation. If this is all that so violent an opposition can bring forward against a cause, the cause must be a wise one. It has seemed to me a certain but a distant event; if, however, Dr. Todd can, in the language of one of his admirers, be induced to reconsider his determination to write no more, it is not impossible that we may count the female vote at the next Presidential election! But towards female suffrage, in itself considered, I have never been able to feel otherwise than indifferent. There are so many things so infinitely more important, more close to the welfare and happiness of society and of individuals, and especially is the happiness of woman so apart from, and independent of, her right of suffrage, that it has seemed an altogether secondary and unimportant matter. Woman without the ballot may possess every condition of a dignified womanhood. Every reason for withholding the ballot from her seems simply frivolous; but what is there on the other side so attractive, so promising, what is there to arouse so much enthusiasm and enlist so many energies? It would sometimes seem, from the tone of discussion, as if the ballot were a sort of talisman, with a power to ward off all harm from its possessor. To me it looks rather like a clumsy contrivance for bringing opinion to bear on government, —fine, delicate, precise, as compared with the old-time method of the sword; but coarse, blundering, and insufficient when compared with the pen, the fireside, and the thousand subtile social influences, penetrating, pervasive, purifying. A few salient points of opinion the ballot-box grasps and presents. A sort of rough, average justice it dispenses, and is so far a powerful influence for good; but all the delicate shades of opinion and all the delicate grades of justice it misses and must always miss. Voting is the prescribed, legal, official way of expressing opinion, but there are many other ways equally powerful.

When it is argued that women should not vote because they are already sufficiently represented by their husbands, brothers, and sons, it may justly be replied that self-appointed representation is no representation at all. If women, with perfect freedom of choice, choose that these men shall vote for them, they may properly be said to be represented; but for man to usurp their vote, and then call himself their representative, is simply falsehood and tyranny. Women might, with precisely the same show of reason, claim the vote on the ground that men would be sufficiently represented by their mothers, wives, and daughters. But is not that which is logically and technically false actually true? Women are not technically represented by men; but is not the opinion of the women of the country really presented with as much accuracy by the actual male vote as it would be by the female vote? Does any one suppose that if female suffrage were established in any State to-day, the vote would be materially changed? Would the Republican party or the Democratic party be larger in relation to its rival than it is now? Is it not true that, as a general thing, the women of a family are, and always will be, of the same political faith as the men of a family? Or we may put it the other way, and say the men of a family always think as the women do,—not necessarily from subserviency on either side, but from the great natural law that birds of a feather flock together. The contrary is sometimes assumed. Female suffrage is opposed on the ground that it would disturb the harmony of families. That is, women must not be allowed to speak, because they will oppose men. This is tyranny pure and simple. It shows that the light parts on our maps are a delusion, and that we are still in barbarism. But I do not think the harmony of families would be disturbed. We know that in religion, which is equally the "sphere" of both sexes, there is little disturbance. Many husbands indifferent to religion have wives who are interested in it, but it is seldom that a positive aggressive Universalist and a similar Orthodox are yoked together. When there is any marked religious leaning, husband and wife usually lean one way. What difference does it make then whether the male and female thought be represented by one vote or two? Now the one Republican vote is met by the one Democratic vote of the neighbor over the way. Then the two Republican votes will be met by the two Democratic votes; but the result will not be changed. There will be a few Democratic wives of Republican husbands, but there will be also a few Republican wives of Democratic husbands.

Women in not voting are not unrepresented in the sense or to the extent to which non-voting negroes are unrepresented. The African is a separate race from the Caucasian, with its own ambitions and traditions. Either, without the other, is an entire and a distinct race; but the men and women of an American community are one race. Either sex alone is but a fragment. Neither rises or falls without taking the other with it. The male vote does not represent male thought alone; it is the product of both male and female thinking. The life of our men and women is constantly and inextricably intertwined; in the house, in the church, in the assembly, in work and worship and recreation, they are inseparable companions, every moment giving and receiving influence. They are so closely joined that their reciprocal relations are the most powerful and important relations of life. So the man represents the woman because he needs must; and he is equally represented by the woman. In any community the character of either sex may be inferred from that of the other. The very laws that bear so unjustly on woman represent not only a man's thought of woman, but woman's thought of herself. If the women of Massachusetts, or of New York, or of any State where there are unjust laws, should rise in a body as women and demand the repeal of those laws, they would be repealed. Strong as are love of power, and the might of brute force, and the greed of gain, there is no man and no law that can stand out against the concentrated will of women. It is because the mass of women do not know what the laws are, or do not care, that the laws stand. The improvement in laws respecting women since the Woman's Rights agitation commenced shows what can be done even by a few women without the ballot. This no more militates against the vote of women than against the vote of men; but, if true, it shows that, when either sex votes, the other does in some sense vote with it. It is not the legislators alone, it is the Woman's Rights women who have been at work repealing old laws and enacting new. Let the women of America make up their minds what laws they want, and they will have them, and may laugh at the ballot.

It is utterly irrational to have scores and hundreds of illiterate foreigners, just naturalized, go to the polls and send one of their own number to make laws for the nation, while an educated and intelligent woman is not allowed to cast a vote to keep him at home. But I see no measure intended to keep the ignorant man away from the polls; only a proposition to enable him to bring his ignorant wife with him. We are not planning to order up a reserved force of intelligence to bear upon unintelligence; for the unintelligence is to order up its reserves just as freely; and the two reserves must pound away at each other, leaving the original forces precisely where they were before. Nor is it true in politics, as in war, that the two trained and intelligent allies are more than a match for their untrained opponents. Patrick's vote has precisely the same power as Mr. Percy Howard's, and Bridget's will count for just as much as Mrs. Percy Howard's; and in everything except the vote intelligence has full play now. Nay, if there is any advantage, I believe it is on the side of Patrick. It is easier to command the vote of the ignorant in a body for the wrong, than that of the wise in a body for the right.

If women say all this is speculation and irrelevant, that they have a right to vote and wish to exercise it, the argument is valid. The burden of proof lies with those who deny the existence and the exercise of this right. I deny neither, but only attempt to show that it is a subordinate and comparatively insignificant matter.

How will the possession of the ballot affect in any way the vexed question of work and wages? One orator says: "Shall Senators tell me in their places that I have no need of the ballot, when forty thousand women in the city of New York alone are earning their daily bread at starving prices with the needle?" But what will the ballot do for those forty thousand women when they get it? It will not give them husbands, nor make their thriftless husbands provident, nor their invalid husbands healthy. They cannot vote themselves out of their dark, unwholesome sewing-rooms into counting-rooms and insurance offices, nor have they generally the qualifications which these places require. The ballot will not enable them to do anything for which their constitution or their education has not fitted them, and I do not know of any law now which prevents them from doing anything for which they are fitted, except the holding of government offices. I can think of no other occupation which the right of suffrage will open to woman, and of public officers the number must always be, in proportion to the population, insignificant. If, as is affirmed, politics is "out of her sphere," if, as I should say, and as I certainly believe, the nature of woman inclines her to private and domestic, rather than to public life, the women who will fill the higher offices will be very few; and, after the subordinate offices are filled, the bulk of the female population will still remain to be provided for. It could hardly be otherwise without calamity. Says a female writer: "How many doors to remunerative employments would be thrown open to woman if she had the ballot!

How politicians would interest themselves in finding places for her!" But I can only say, far distant be that day! If the possession of the ballot is to enlist woman in the great army of office-seekers, it will be a disastrous possession both to herself and the state. I cannot look upon such a sentiment from a woman without dismay. Are women to be elevated by becoming entangled with politicians and intriguing for places? Are men thus elevated? Is it generally considered a creditable and honorable employment for men to be hanging upon the skirts of Congressmen? Finding places for her! I trust the ballot, if it does anything, will enable woman to command place for herself. I trust that the mischievous doctrine that places are to be found for persons, and not persons for places, will receive no countenance from women. The enormous losses in purse and reputation already sustained by the country from the incompetence and dishonesty of her servants are sufficiently appalling. So far as women have any influence, let them teach that the honor, the prosperity, the resources of the country are a sacred trust, to be committed to the most worthy, not a huge treasure-trove to be plundered by the most needy and greedy. For women, if office they are to have, I pray let office always seek them, but let them never seek office.

Is it said that the impetus given to woman by the social elevation consequent on the possession of the ballot will act in every direction, will quicken all her energies, will impel her into a thousand paths which now she never dreams of entering, and will give her an importance in the eyes of men which will effectually secure her from their oppression?

But how is this work to be wrought? Does the possession of the ballot really mark any practical social elevation for women? Will they stand, either in their own view or in that of men, any higher? Will they have more social influence, or, if their vote be the duplicate of the male vote, will they have any separate political influence? The vote in the hands of the freedman marks a real change. He was a slave; he is a man, and the ballot is at once the sign and the staff of his freedom. But women are free-born. They have an acknowledged, or at least an uncontested right to form and to express opinions on every subject, in every way that man has, save one. Much real power of expression, much actual influence, they possess which men do not. They have no consciousness of inferiority. Those women who are wise and thoughtful, who understand politics, political and historical, and who comprehend situations, are too high to be degraded by the absence of the ballot. Classing them with idiots does not make them idiots. The classification fixes the status of the classifiers, not of the classified. Their rank and power in society, and their self-respect, will not be touched by suffrage. The influence of any woman's vote is slight compared with that of her voice. As for the feeble and frivolous women, — the women who are given over to trivialities, who know and care nothing for politics, and reckon their ignorance an accomplishment,—will the ballot raise them up into dignified human beings? I hope so. It is, indeed, almost the only ground of hope; it is almost the only direction in which there seems to be a prospect of any definite advantage from female suffrage; but I fear not. If women can live in the midst of the deep, strong excitement of the times, if their ears can be filled with the discussion of questions which affect the honor and safety of the country, and yet brain and heart remain untouched, there is reason to fear that the franchise will fail to enfranchise them. All this is no reason for withholding it. I only intimate that such withholding cannot be considered the cause of the apathy which prevails, and that the bestowal of the ballot will hardly dispel the apathy. It is only that the ballot has no power to elevate those who are unworthy to hold it. The "mobs and rowdies" have long held the ballot, but are no less mobs and rowdies. The ballot neither elevates nor depresses. It takes its character from its possessor.

What incitement to honor, profit, education, do women miss in missing the ballot? What barrier will it remove, what stimulus present? The brilliant prizes of life are already open to female competition. There are still unequal laws, but not so many, or so severe, as to prevent any woman's becoming whatever she has power to become in any walk of life except the political. Within her grasp lies all the freedom which she has the nerve to secure. Prejudice itself has softened down into an insipidity which is no obstacle to a really robust soul. There may be petty jealousies to impede and annoy, but these the ballot will not remove; and these excellence, without the ballot, will remove. Art, literature, science, theology, medicine, — all lie in her manor, but how largely are they left uncultivated! Miss Dickinson has had a career more brilliant than that of most men, but she stands almost alone upon the platform. Miss Hosmer's position is honorable and secure, but her followers are few. Mrs. Stowe has left all men far behind her, but the female story-writers are no better than they were before Uncle Tom came, and spoke, and conquered. What has the ballot to do with such women? It can give them no more money, for they already command the highest market-price. It can give them no social standing, for they rank first now. Does the want of it keep any one from adopting their career? I venture to say that there is not at this moment in the whole country a woman who is held back from public speaking, or from any of the finer or higher arts, for lack of voting. If women held to-morrow the right of suffrage, there would not be any more female lawyers, preachers, artists, doctors, than there are to-day. The opponents of female suffrage think otherwise. Strongly declaring that these things are repugnant to womanhood, they profess to believe that no sooner is woman absolutely free than she at once rushes into them; that is, the moment nature has scope, it turns upon itself. But I believe that women do, and always will, of their own choice, prefer seclusion to publicity; for they have now sufficient freedom of choice to indicate this. There is nothing now to hinder a woman from taking charge of a church, if she and the church wish it. Indeed, women to-day hold pastorates, and no one molests them. Probably there is not a village or a city in New England where a woman would not be listened to respectfully, and given full credit for all her wit and wisdom. Let any woman, who is moved to address a public assembly, announce such an intention, and she will have a larger audience than a man of similar ability, and she will have at least an equally appreciative hearing. If she can sustain herself, she will be sustained by the public.

Is it said that women are not yet educated to fill these public positions, and therefore they do not come forward? But every school, except the highest, is open to girls now; and even the doors of colleges are beginning to creak on their hinges. The self-same day on which women wish to go to college, they will go. While men are hesitating, colleges are founding for women; but if a force of sixty girls, well fitted for college, should beleaguer old Harvard to-day, they would compel her to capitulate. Nay, if twenty girl-graduates of high schools should knock at her doors for admission, those doors might groan and grate harsh thunder, but they would swing open, and let them in. Meanwhile, I suppose our high schools are quite equal to the colleges of fifty years ago, so that girls now may have as good an education as their grandfathers, and really their grandfathers made a very respectable figure.

I am willing to admit that our girls generally are not half educated, but I fail to see how the ballot is responsible for the deficiency. This is no reason why the ballot should be refused them, but it is a reason why they need not be listless and miserable without it. It is a reason why we may not attribute our lack of female orators, artists, writers, and speakers to its absence.

Still we have not reached the masses, — the women who have no inward, irresistible bent to anything, who have no ambition for a career, but who must earn their own living, who, while the leaders are conquering all opposition, all circumstances, still remain, thirty-nine thousand

and five hundred out of forty thousand, for whose sake the ballot is demanded, and whose fortunes the ballot is expected to create. We have as yet found no answer to the question, What will the ballot do for them? A thousand employments it will give them, say its advocates, but they do not specify ten. Indeed, I cannot find one. Is it, in fact, the want of the ballot that keeps them at starving prices, any more than it is the want of the ballot that keeps them back from art and science? I think not. All suffering is pitiable, but I cannot spend all my pity on these forty thousand. I pity myself. I pity the twice forty thousand women in New York who are annoyed, hindered, and injured by the incapacity of foreign servants that do not know the difference between a castor and a tureen, or between truth and falsehood; but whose lives might grow smooth and peaceful through the advent of forty thousand intelligent American servants. These forty thousand women are starving over their needles, but if a busy house-mother wants a plain dress made, she must pay ten dollars for the work, bespeak it a month beforehand at that, and submit to whatever abstraction of pieces the dress-maker or her apprentices choose to make. Not to speak of dress-making, it is no easy matter to secure really good plain sewing; and really good plain sewing, so far as I know, always commands good pay. Why then do not these women who are starving over the needle make fine dresses for twenty dollars, instead of coarse trousers for twenty cents? Why do they not become milliners and mantua-makers, and earn a fortune and an independent position, instead of remaining slop-makers, earning barely a living, and never rising above a servile and cringing dependence? It is because they have not the requisite skill or money; but of these they cannot vote themselves a supply. Here is a girl who wants some other work than sewing. She goes to a counting-room, and is offered, by way of trial, a package of letters to copy. The work is expected to occupy about a week, and she is to be paid twenty-five dollars. She brings back the letters, copied in a clear, round hand, but so carelessly and inaccurately that her work is worthless. Here is a pretty, bright young woman, engaged with a roomful of companions in a similar work, and actually boasting that her employers "cannot do anything with us. They make rules that we are to be here at such times, and to leave the room only at such times, and do only such and such things; but we will do just as we like"; and I am not surprised by and by to hear that there is trouble brewing, nor do I see how the right of suffrage is to remove the trouble. There are so many things to be taken into the account, that one has need of great caution in forming opinions; but it seems to me that the great and simple cause of the low wages paid to women is the low work they produce. They are equal only to the coarse, common labor; they get only the coarse, common pay, and there are such multitudes of them that their employer has everything his own way. The moment they rise to a higher grade of work, the crowd thins, and they become masters of the situation. It may not be their fault that they are not skilled artisans, but I suppose trade takes into account only facts, not causes. I am not now exculpating or inculpating those who grind the faces of the poor. I am not speaking of them at all. I desire and design to look at the question solely from the woman's point of view. The laws of supply and demand are just as rigorous as if the brutal and profane head-shopman were a wooden automaton. There are a few employers who modify them by moral laws; but to the great mass work is worth just what it can be got for, and so long as work can be got at starving prices, living prices will not be paid. What can the ballot do here? Nothing but mischief. The relations between employer and employed the law seldom touches but to disturb. "Hands off" is all we want of government, — its own hands and all others. Freedom, not fostering, is its aim, — or fostering only through freedom. Only so far as government continually tends to non-government, continually tends to relegate its power to the individual, to decrease itself and to increase the citizen, is it performing the true function of government.

But if women are prevented from establishing themselves in business through want of means, they need not on that account work at starving prices. I suspect that every one of those forty thousand women could find a comfortable home in New York, — a home in which she would have plenty of wholesome food and sufficient shelter, and in which she could earn besides two or three dollars a week, if she would accept the home. The work would be more healthful and far less exhaustive than the starvation sewing. Household service is always in demand. A woman needs no capital to enter upon it. Even skill is not indispensable. There are thousands of families to which, if an intelligent, virtuous, and ordinarily healthful woman should go and say, "I have been starving with my needle, and I desire now to try housework. I know very little about it, but I have determined to devote myself to it, and am resolved to become mistress of it," she would be welcomed. Here, by exercising those virtues and graces which every human being ought to exercise,—by being faithful, good-humored, and efficient,—she could speedily become an honored and valued member of the family, and secure herself a home that would last as long as the family held together. She could make herself as useful to the family as the family is to her. Where is the sense in a woman's starving because she has no food in her hands, when a woman is starving by her side because she has no hands for her food? I feel indignant when I hear these multiplied stories of wholesale destitution. I am disposed to say to these women: If you choose to stay at home and perish, rather than go into your neighbor's kitchen and supply your wants, do so; but do not appeal to those for pity from whom you refuse employment. I know there are many who are tied to their own wretched homes; but if those who are unencumbered would resort to the kitchens of the rich, it would relieve the stress of competition, those who remain would command a better price for their labor, and starvation would be permanently stopped. I do not say this because housework is woman's sphere, but because it is honest work that calls her, and any honest work in her power is better than starvation, and more dignified than complaint and outcry. If it were picking apples, or gathering huckleberries, instead of housework, I should recommend that just the same. The case of the woman is precisely the case of the man. If a man had palpable artistic genius, we should earnestly desire for him artistic employment; but if he could by no means succeed in securing it, we should certainly advise him to chop wood, however disagreeable wood-chopping be to him, rather than die; and if he chose to shiver and starve at his home, rather than come and cut my wood, for want of which I stand shivering, I should take his starvation with great equanimity. So with women. No one has a right to tell women what they ought to do, to dictate to them their sphere. But when women cry out that they are dying for want of the ballot, we have a right to say: Not so. Unquestionably you are dying, and unquestionably you have not the ballot; but the two do not stand in the relation of effect and cause. Equally without question you ought to have the ballot; but it is not the ballot which will raise you up from this sickness.

I admit that there are serious drawbacks to household service,—some drawbacks of an honest self-respect, some of a foolish self-disrespect, calling itself pride. It is often said, that, if a woman could be taken into a family on a footing of equality,—meaning chiefly, I find, if she could sit at the family table,—there would be less reluctance to domestic service. It is not reasonable to expect that an intelligent American woman should be willing to consort with low and ignorant foreigners. But it would scarcely be hazardous to predict, that, if intelligent American women would go into American kitchens, they would quickly drive out the unintelligent foreigners; and for the rest, the matter of equality is simply trivial. Social position adjusts itself where there is social worth. The servant in the kitchen may be wholly superior to the mistress in the parlor, or she may be inferior; but sitting together at table affects the question not at all. It may be requiring more insight than we have a right to expect, to ask the mass of women to see this. But any one can see that the table is often the only place where the family can meet, and a stranger's presence destroys the confidence and freedom which make the charm of family life. The family do not object to the servant's presence necessarily because she is not equal to themselves, but because she is not one of themselves. They are quite right. Family seclusion can scarcely be too sacredly guarded; and the woman who wishes to encroach upon it — who is so blind that she cannot see that there is anything to be encroached upon — shows by that token her unfitness to share it. There is, too, much less danger of clashing when mistress and maid have their orbits on different planes. Duties are far more clearly defined, and relations far less complicated; and if the maid have ability, she will gradually assume an almost commanding position in the household. She will be less its servant than its friend, its care-taker, honored and prized beyond what money can express.

But there is also, it must be admitted, a well-grounded repugnance to household service because of the character of the householders. There are women who seem to have no suspicion that servants have any rights, tastes, or feelings which mistresses are bound to respect. They are exacting and petulant. They make no allowance for human nature. They take no thought for the comfort, the health, or the welfare of their servants, but expect the servant to take constant thought for theirs. It never occurs to them that a servant has any need of rest or recreation, of society or sunshine. They consider the servant an absolute dependant, and themselves ab solute monarchs. Perhaps there is no remedy for this but to let such women alone. And yet, at the worst, are the selfishness and unreason of a mistress worse than those of a master? Possibly. More petty, constant, and irritating, perhaps, but not so brutal, so repulsive. At the worst, are the small rooms, the close kitchens, the constant calls, worse than the long monotonous days spent over the health- and heart-destroying needle? But the worst cases are comparatively few, though they bring all others into bad odor. The actually good places are not few, and the passable places are many, and will be more, just as fast as good women can be found to fill them. Let intelligence and modesty and worth go into the kitchen, and they must soon bring intelligence and modesty and worth into the parlor. There is also another advantage for young women: while all their copying or shop-keeping has no peculiar value except as a trade, housework is an apprenticeship which may be very useful to them in a different position. They are not only gaining money, comfort, and independence, but they are fitting themselves for keeping their own houses, if they shall ever have houses to keep. With their one stone they are hitting all the birds they will ever be likely to have a chance at.

I do not mean to say that this backwardness about entering household service is entirely owing to indisposition. Much, doubtless, is due to the fact that supply does not know how to get at demand. The women who are bending over the needle are not able to be far or clear sighted, and they see nothing else to do but to live on from hand to mouth. They cannot give up their sewing long enough to seek places. They have no capital to live on while in search of them. There is a pathos in the fact that a single advertisement a short time since, as I happen to know, brought nearly three hundred answers; and the advertiser secured, not only for himself but for several friends, admirable domestic assistants. This, at least, is certain; in a country where the conditions of life are as equal as in ours, and where the male population is always in excess of the female, there is not the slightest need of any woman's starving for want of remunerative work. But the irregularity or absence of communication between those who want work done and those who want to do work, is a matter for individual enterprise, rather than for legislative enactment. The establishment of a bureau to supply the defect, and bring the two pressing wants face to face, would seem to be a fine object of philanthropic activity, and very likely of business ability. To wait for the ballot to do this is worthy of the subjects of an Oriental absolutism, not of the citizens of a great Republic.

What can the ballot do towards equalizing wages, where work is already equalized without affecting wages, as is not unfrequently the case? There are shops of the same sort, on the same street, with male clerks in one and female clerks in another, where the former work fewer hours and receive higher wages than the latter. There is a wrong, an injustice, but the law cannot interfere. It cannot force a haberdasher to pay ten dollars for service which he can secure for six. Moreover, the question of female clerkship is not yet settled. There are conscientious, intelligent, and obliging shopkeepers, who say that female clerks are not satisfactory. Their strength is not equal to the draughts made upon it. They are not able to stand so long as clerks are required to stand. They have not the patience, the civility, the tact that male clerks have. I do not know how this is; I only say these things are alleged. I have never noticed any especial incivility in female clerks, and I see no objection to their sitting when they have nothing to do. But the persons who hire are the persons to require and to define service, and if they do not choose girls, or do not value them so highly as boys, how can legislation help it? All the voting in the world can never add a cubit to a woman's stature. Here also the rule of quantity and quality comes into play, and regulates wages with a high hand. So long as ten girls stand before the door for every one girl that stands behind the counter, ready to take the place which she relinquishes for the self-same wages that she disdains, there is very little use in talking; but superior business qualifications are recognized and rewarded. Waiting in the office of one of our large business establishments not long since, I observed a young woman open the door and report a telegraphic question to the proprietor. He gave her an oral answer to be transmitted by telegraph, and when she had gone he said to me: "There is not another person in the house to whom I would trust a telegram unwritten. She is sure to be accurate. *An intelligent woman is more intelligent than an intelligent man.*" I said: "How do her wages compare with those of a man?" "We pay her just as we should pay a man."

But teaching, which is admitted to be a peculiarly feminine employment, and which under male regulations is attended with most flagrant injustice, is chiefly a public concern. It belongs to the State, it is adjusted by the ballot, and its injustice is therefore a proper subject of legislative control. That there is injustice it is hardly possible to deny. Not only is a woman paid less than a man for the same service, but in a public school a woman will be substituted for a man on the ground that she is a better teacher; her superiority to him is recognized as the cause of her appointment over him; and yet she will receive only about two thirds of his salary. A woman teaches in a high school, side by side with a man, and knows that she does more work and better work than he, and that she is acknowledged to do it, and yet receives less than one half, often not more than one third, as much as he receives. Will female suffrage remedy this? If it could be changed by voting, would the votes of women change it? Is there any reason to suppose that women would be any more forward than men in paying high wages to a woman? Are women, as a general thing, more ready than men to do justice to a woman? I fear not. There are women who deprecate this state of things, but there are also men. The mass of men are willing it should be as it is, but so are the mass of women. I think, if the women of a country village were to decide by vote whether the schoolmistress in summer should have as much a month as the schoolmaster in winter, the money coming from their own, that is, their husbands' purses, they would vote, No, in about the same proportion as men now vote it. If the women in a city ward were asked whether the female assistants in their high schools should have as much as the male, they also would largely answer, No. It is partly because women have not sufficient *esprit de corps* to stand up for one another to any extent. Women's love of men is so much stronger than their love of justice, that they would go wrong with men, rather than right, against them. So far as this is the result of a false education, of God-is-thy-law-thou-mine teachings, it is to be deprecated. So far as it is the natural arrangement of things, it is beneficial. Certainly that would be a calamitous cause which should array the two sexes against each other. I trust we shall never be reduced to such extremities that women must band together to extort justice from men, as the bold barons extorted Magna Charta from King John. It would, in fact, be practically impossible, for the idea underlying the relation of the two sexes is the idea of unity; that of individuals of either sex is separation; and this instinct of unity will always keep men and women working with and for each other, though they may often work wrong. So much the more reason is there that they should learn to work right, — that their mutual helpfulness should not be perverted into mutual hindrance, — that tyranny on the one side and subserviency on the other should not usurp the moral support which is due to each sex from the other. As it is, women have no better friends than some men, and no worse foes than many women.

Another reason for supposing that female suffrage will not change the status is that women do not seem generally to quarrel with the status. They are just as free to speak their minds now as they will be to vote their minds by and by; and except from teachers and their immediate friends, I do not recollect hearing any remonstrance against the inequality of the wages of teachers. Women generally look upon it with apparent indifference. It scarcely excites remark, and an exposition of the wrong meets only a languid assent. Even teachers themselves usually take very little notice of it. Girls accept summer schools and summer wages without protest or comment, and are only too glad of them. But few teachers, and those of the highest character, express any dissent.

What would be the use? The State, like any private employer, pays market prices for its work, and the machinery works all the more smoothly because people do not know the difference between a good article and a poor one. If a clergyman preaches dull sermons, or a tailor makes an ill-fitting coat, — if a doctor loses patients and a lawyer cases, — their sin finds them out at once. Not so with a poor teacher. He may go on in his poorness for years, and never be found out. If a teacher is popular, his employers are satisfied; if he is unpopular, they are dissatisfied. The best teacher will always be liked by his pupils, but an unpopular teacher may be vastly better than a popular one. The popular qualities may be joined with vices of character whose debasing influences will go with the pupils through life, and the unpopular qualities may be allied with sterling virtues whose effect will be equally strong and durable. People do not consider their children of so much importance as what they call business. Women who will not let a week, scarcely a day, pass without inspecting their kitchens; men who keep every branch of their business under their own eye, will let their children go to school by the year together without any personal acquaintance with the teachers under whom they are placed, or any personal knowledge of the method pursued in their education. In what is really the most important concern of their lives, they trust entirely to others. The co-operation, even the communication, between parents and teachers is generally next to nothing.

As a timely illustration of the condition of things, let me state a fact which once came under my observation.

In a New England city somewhat famous for its schools, it was publicly announced that a professor of elocution would give a course of lectures to the teachers. At the time appointed, a goodly number of teachers were assembled; and a member of the school committee, a clergyman, called the meeting to order, and said to them, in substance: "We obtained Professor Blank's services to instruct the teachers, because we felt you needed it. Could you have heard all that was said by the committee regarding the reading in your schools, at the time this matter was under consideration, you would not feel flattered. The committee *wish* they had it in their power to *insist* on the attendance of every teacher at these lectures. As one of the grammar masters remarked, if any teacher does not feel sufficiently interested to attend, her place had better be filled by one who does! Let me say, though we have it not in our power to insist on every one's attending, yet the committee expect every teacher to attend, and if there are those who do not, *they will be remembered!*"

I think that the existence in a community of any correct idea of the teacher's character, position, and functions would have prevented such a display of "plantation manners." It would make it impossible for a community to choose, as the medium of communication between itself and its teachers, a man capable of the combined churlishness and cowardice of this clergyman. Or, if he should creep into office, it would make it impossible for him to exercise his cowardice and churlishness by singling out the female teachers for insult, while adroitly exonerating by implication the male teachers, who, as it was his business to know, are equally responsible. It would shed, even through his brain, some glimmering consciousness that a body of teachers whom it was fit thus to address were persons totally unfit to be intrusted with the education of children, and that therefore the blame of their shortcomings would rest with the community that employed them; and it would thus prevent a good deed from being barbarously marred in the doing.

If, then, a good teacher should refuse anything less than a man's salary, she would simply be discarded, and a substitute found. The substitute might be inferior, but her employers would never know it. How can a workman, with any expectation of success, demand high wages on the ground of high work, when his employer does not know the difference between high work and low? More than this, employers value high work so little that they do not even demand the external conditions without which high work is not to be expected. Public opinion does not demand that female teachers should be educated, and in consequence a large proportion of them are uneducated. That is, the intellectual training of children is committed to persons who are themselves almost entirely deficient in what would properly be called intellectual training. If a person is conversant with the branches which he is called upon to teach, it is enough. The effect upon mind and heart which education gives is not held in estimation. A high-school teacher must know Latin and mathematics and history, not because he is any broader and better man for the knowledge, but because he must teach these studies. A primary-school teacher does not teach them. So a girl who does not know enough to enter as pupil the lowest class of a high school may enter the primary school as teacher. Parents are quite satisfied to intrust their young children to persons who earn no more, and who receive no more, than the cook in the kitchen. That is, it is considered fitting and economical to consign children at the most susceptible age — at the age when they are the least influenced by books and most by personal contact with the teacher — to the care of an ignorant and almost unknown person. At the time when the teacher's character has the most influence, it is considered of the least importance; while, when girls and boys are pretty thoroughly moulded, it is thought necessary to employ teachers with some pretensions to learning. There needs a different and a deeper change than any proposed by the ballot. It needs to be understood that the instruction of children in their early years is at least as important and as exacting as that in their later years. It needs to be understood that their early education requires not only as peculiar a fitness, but as elaborate a preparation, as their later education. If a woman has natural skill and tact, she needs education to give weight to her teaching and material for her tact. Her work in the primary school exhausts just as much vital force, makes just as large a drain upon her intellectual resources, and should receive just as high remuneration, as work in the high school. To raise the standard of wages, without raising the standard of qualifications, would be but premature reform.. A great many female teachers already receive more than they are worth. They are not fit for their places. It is not their fault. They are faithful enough, as far as they know. Parents employ them and are content with what service they render; but, compared with what teachers ought to be and to do, they are good for nothing. The same is true of men, — though perhaps not so largely. The proportion of male teachers who have received a liberal education is very much larger than that of female teachers. But if it were smaller, it would make no difference. That a male teacher is bad, does not make a female teacher good. That a man is receiving ten times as much as he is worth, does not make a woman worth what she receives. That a woman is worth far more than a man, does not make her worth what she would be if she were educated. Let the standard be raised, and the number of competitors is at once diminished, and we are in the line of higher wages. But I have no expectation of any palpable or permanent relative increase in the wages of female teachers until female resources are multiplied. When women are able to refuse low wages, they will be offered high wages. So long as they are glad of ever so small remuneration, they will be sure to get it. When female teachers are so good, so strong, so facile, so able to turn their hands to something else, that if they cannot get good wages for teaching they will follow an occupation in which they can get good wages, the work is done. They will need no ballot to be in demand. As it is, they are at the mercy of their employers. If a girl is ever so disgusted with her two or three hundred dollars a year, she does not know which way to turn to get more. She must take what people choose to pay; and will people ever choose to pay more than they are obliged to pay?

The difference in the number of occupations pursued by men and those pursued by women has less practical effect on women's wages than mere statistics indicate. The men who are disposed of by employments not open or not possible to women, must be pretty well matched by the women who are engaged in the employments which are ordinarily involved in marriage, and which are equally shut to men. So that the number of women and of men left to compete for the employments common to both cannot be so very unequal; and their wages would not naturally be very dissimilar. Nor can the existing dissimilarity be owing to the greater number of women than of men in the country, for there are by actual count more men than women. So far as it arises from an unequal distribution of women, the inequality may be remedied by bureaus of employment, by individual energy, by private philanthropy, by anything except law. An error in the calculation may be that marriage does not entirely withdraw women from the competitive employments. It ought to do so. Every married woman, especially every mother, ought to be able to devote her whole working time to her domestic duties.

The care and labor of a family, with or without children, are enough for any one woman. Every married woman who, not forced by natural taste and aptitude, but by outward necessity, the *res angusta domi*, engages in money-earning occupation, is a monument of her husband's incompetency, — always excepting illness, which is incompetency, indeed, though perhaps of the least reprehensible sort. Any person with a just idea of what is due to a family and from a family knows that the family occupation is absorbing and exclusive. The danger indeed is that it will absorb that to which it has no right, and exclude that which is its sacred duty; but in the matter of employment it bears, like the Turk, no brother near the throne. Still I do not know that a law could be passed prohibiting married women from binding shoes, or knitting sale stockings, or teaching school. We must take things as they are, bending them always towards the right. As things are, if women would make a wise choice of work, and would thoroughly fit themselves for the positions which they choose, I see no reason why they should not materially mend their condition. If the women whose natural endowments fit them, and whose natural taste leads them, to be teachers would fortify their endowments by corresponding acquisitions, would correct and cultivate their taste by a long course of intellectual training,—if the women whose bent is to book-keeping and business would take pains to understand book-keeping and business, would carry to them the same attention and devotion which men carry,—if the women to whom housekeeping is of itself no more distasteful than school-keeping, who would never think of declining marriage because it involved housekeeping, but would rather look forward with pleasure to that feature of it, — if they would put away false pride and keep a house not their own, would not a relief be felt in every part of the social system? When it is found that the women who have not the power or the taste to become trained and valued teachers have become trained housewives, or skilful seamstresses, or accomplished laundresses, or sweetmeat-makers, or strawberry-fanciers, or counting-room clerks, and the supply of teachers is somewhat scant, there will be no drawing back on account of a few hundred dollars more or less. And the laundresses and housewives will have a less exhaustive, a more satisfactory life, and a more remunerative occupation, than they had as poor teachers.

Does not this require a change other than the ballot can accomplish, — other indeed than the ballot proposes to accomplish,—but a change entirely possible of accomplishment without the ballot?

Meanwhile, let the underpaid teachers console themselves with the reflection that they are doing the community ten times more harm by bad work than the community is doing them by bad pay!

What will woman's vote do to reform our criminal code? Everything, say some. Vice, if we may trust these rosy-hued visions, is to disappear when women hold the ballot. I anticipate no such result. Vice is too deeply rooted in men's hearts to be extirpated by any such summary process. Crime is hardly repressed by legislation; vice, never. That attempts will be made I do not doubt. Men have made them to some extent. Women, with a moral sense more keen in some directions, if more obtuse from want of cultivation in others, will renew the attempt with a more eager effort, and doubtless with a temporary and local success. The royal road to a desired object will seem to be legislation, and legislation we shall have in galore. But the principles of human nature, which are the principles of Divine truth, are unchangeable, and if we do not work in line with them our work will come to naught. Every human law not founded on natural law must sooner or later fall to the ground. If it is a natural law that no man shall interfere with his fellow except to prevent his interference with his fellows, a law establishing such interference will be both useless and harmful. If moral ends can be attained by moral means alone, legislative enactments will be none the less impertinent and invalid because they are framed from benevolent motives. A knowledge of the successes and failures of other nations and ages would be of great service to us in solving the problems of our own. A knowledge of political and social principles would do much towards guiding our thinking into right channels. But such knowledge is the very last to be found. Here the principle of representation is carried out with marvellous fidelity. The dense popular ignorance, not only of the nature but of the existence of such a science as political economy, is ably and fully represented in every legislative assembly, State and National. The result is visible in laws that perish with the using; but often not till they have spread derangement and distress through every class on which they are brought to bear. We try experiments on abandoned theories, with an alacrity and a confidence which imply a most touching ignorance of the fact that some points are settled. It is hardly probable that women are any better qualified for legislation than men. As they have never been held to public responsibility for their opinions, they have perhaps taken less trouble to form correct ones; as there has always been in the inferior male mind a certain repugnance to the possession by women of any political knowledge, and therefore a certain odium attached to such possession, it may well be that women are at present even less fitted to legislate wisely than many men. More unfit than many men they cannot be, for multitudes appear to have no single qualification to insure wise legislative action. From the access of women to the ballot-box, therefore, we may look for a sword before peace.

Nothing need be feared from this. It is natural that woman should have part in government, and therefore the consequence must be good. Moreover, if the ballot ever educates, it will educate women. If women are not far enough advanced to be improved by it, who is? But though it will be better in the end, because it is the only rational way of doing things, at first we shall have rather more crude law-making, rather more legislative journey-work, than we have now. Women will attempt to sweep away vice with the besom of law, and with apparent success. But a reaction will follow, and into the empty, swept, and garnished house will enter seven devils more wicked than the first. Then the evil will correct itself, and so the pendulum will swing back and forth, till the united trials of men and women will, we hope, teach them that the motives and the character of law-makers will not give efficiency to that law which is not founded on the eternal principles of nature and truth. Men and women together will be slow to learn it, but they will learn it a little faster than either would alone. Now it is easy to charge every deviation of the ship from her course to the want of a womanly hand at the helm; but when the womanly hand is there, and we see the ship still veering from her track, we shall begin to believe that the trouble lies elsewhere as well, and enter upon an honest and earnest search for its cause. I do not mean that with woman's vote we shall do any worse than we do now. We must, at least after a while, do better. But we shall do so little better, and that little so slowly, that long-time opponents of female suffrage will wag their heads and cry, Aha! Aha! and imagine that they have fully established their reputation for superior, far-sighted wisdom. This is of small account. The fact will remain that the one bone of contention, the one root of bitterness between man and woman, will be removed. This of itself, even if no principle of justice were involved, might seem enough to warrant the extension of the suffrage to woman, and is a result to be counted on with more certainty than any immediate improvement of the laws. If men believe as firmly as they profess to believe that they are doing the best which can be done, I should think they would, like the unjust steward, make friends of the mammon of unrighteousness, and say to women: "You fancy you can do so much better than we. Just try it. Take the ballot and convert the world at once to goodness and justice." So long as women have not the ballot, they will fondly picture the things which they might accomplish with it. Give them the ballot, that they may see for themselves how little it can do. Give them the ballot, that they may have all the power there is, and learn its weakness. Give them the ballot, that we may have decided what is the nature of woman, and so reconcile or destroy all conflicting theories of woman's sphere, and learn once for all by her success or failure what purpose her Maker had in her creation. This we certainly never can learn so long as woman either is, or believes herself to be, held back by unjust restrictions.

Somewhat as President Buchanan maintained that the South had no right to go out of the Union, and the North had no right to hinder it; so, as a woman I would never ask the ballot, and as a man I would never refuse it.

Female suffrage appears to be a foregone conclusion; it remains for us to prevent it so far as possible from being a conclusion in which nothing is concluded.

Right or wrong, England and America seem tending towards universal suffrage, and in fact, as in terms, universal suffrage must include female suffrage. Not attempting or desiring to interfere with those who would hasten our steps, I feel more concerned that there should be preparation for it. To me, female suffrage, in the form in which it is proposed, shares with universal suffrage, though in a less degree, the character of an experiment whose result is doubtful. Manhood suffrage has a noble ring to it. But its warmest advocates do not mean precisely what they say. No suffrage is meant to be absolutely universal, absolutely unrestricted. Lunatics are denied it, notwithstanding that the point where sanity ends and insanity begins is often indeterminable. Foreigners are denied it, though no one questions that Count Gasparin, on his arrival in America, would know more of our political philosophy, our practical tendency, and national needs, than an ordinary Irish laborer after a five years' residence. Minors are denied it, but many a lad of eighteen or fifteen, and not a few of twelve years, understand the issues better, and are far more able to vote intelligently, than many of our naturalized citizens. Strictly speaking, then, no one advocates universal suffrage. All are in favor of limitations, and limitations which must often be in their operations somewhat arbitrary, though they are meant to follow, and do largely follow, the great natural lines of distinction. There is therefore nothing unnatural, nothing inconsistent, nothing unrepublican, in an endeavor to restrict still further the suffrage. If society has the right to make one restriction, it has the same abstract right to make another. If it has the right to say that men may vote at twenty-one, but may not vote at twenty, because it is judged that twenty-one is on an average the earliest age at which we may expect discretion, it is not inherently unreasonable and repugnant to common sense and human nature to say that a man shall not vote at twenty-one unless he can read and write. The right and the wrong of it depend upon the nature, not upon the fact, of the restriction. Nor does there seem to be any reason why restrictions upon the suffrage should be of such a nature that mere lapse of time, without any regard to character, shall be sufficient to remove them. I should be glad to see a man required to give some proof of ability before he is allowed to control society. For the ballot does not mean simply self-government; it is also government of others. The vote of New York is not confined to regulating New York interests. It sends John Morrissey to Congress to make laws for the nation, and may send him to the Court of Saint James to represent the nation. The same authority which has a right to say that a man who has been in State prison for crime shall not exercise over others the lordship of voting has a right to say that a man who has not taken the trouble to learn to read the law which forbids crime and prescribes its penalty shall not exercise such lordship. Surely in a country like ours inability to read and write is as strong presumptive evidence of incompetency to exercise the right of suffrage as the fact of being only twenty years old. I should be glad to go further, and not only have the standard of qualification higher, but, notwithstanding the antiquity of the idea, make the possession of the ballot contingent upon the possession of property. Property suffrage has indeed an aristocratic and odious sound, — beside manhood suffrage a mere materialistic tinkle; but government itself we want chiefly for materialistic purposes, chiefly to keep men from preying upon one another, and so give ample room for all idealism and all excellence to flourish. Government deals very largely with property interests, and it seems as if those who earn and dispense property are the ones to understand best the laws which control it. He who cannot manage it for himself is hardly the one to manage it for other people. The aristocracy of property suffrage may be a very democratic aristocracy. In our country the race is open to all. The competitors, as a general thing, carry only such weights as nature imposes. The goal is acknowledged to be fitting, and the laurels worth the wearing. Hence there seems to be no more generally accurate sign of wisdom, thrift, practical ability, than success here. Undoubtedly there are exceptions, but no more than there are to the other rules. The standard need not be high. We do not want a rich man's government, but we do want a wise, a judicious, a responsible man's government; and nothing contributes more to this than the possession of property which depends for its value chiefly upon the nature of the government. The poor man's fifties or hundreds at stake make him as careful, as conservative, as interested, as the rich man's thousands. He will be just as alert against foolish expenditure, just as restless under oppressive taxes. Certainly let the ballot be put within reach of every industrious person in any calling of life; let the condition of suffrage be such that a non-fulfilment of the condition is presumptive evidence of incapacity to exercise the right. Who shall fix the standard? The same authority that fixes it now. The authority that grants to every tatterdemalion the right to vote because he is twenty-one years old may forbid the man of twenty-one years to vote because he is a tatterdemalion. The indiscriminate bestowal of the ballot makes the ballot common and unclean. A restriction of age alone offers no stimulus to improvement. A restriction of sex or color is a barrier to improvement. No incapacity retains the one restriction; no capacity removes the other. I would have the ballot made a noble and desirable possession, a sign of sagacity, of ability, of worth, something to be striven for, a guerdon as well as a power. And when it is thus ennobled, let it be open to all who can fulfil the conditions, — men and women, black and white.

I think men do not dream how aggravated is the affront they put upon women in some of the arguments about voting which they employ. I do not mean such men as Dr. Todd alone, who cannot open their mouths but to exasperate; but men who really know in many respects what they are talking about, who are capable of speaking on the subject with candor and moderation, and not without sense, but who are unhappily not incapable of using arguments utterly beneath the dignity of man or woman, — arguments which, employed towards themselves, they would be the first to resent, and whose fallacy, employed on any other theme, they would swiftly detect and denounce. I mean such responses, to the women who claim right of suffrage, as that women have plenty to do at home without asking office; that they had better do their own work well, before they ask to do men's; that if they would teach poor women and their own daughters to sew well and to cook well, they would have a sufficiently broad field for the exercise of their philanthropy and all their powers, and would do far more good to the country than by voting; that if they persist in demanding their rights so strenuously, they may get more rights than they want, — the right to stand in cars and to take outside seats on coaches. These are the arguments of savages, and fit to be addressed to savages, but they are unworthy of civilized people. To attempt to deter women from claiming what belongs to them by threatening to withhold something which does not belong to them, is child's play, and very small and mean play at that. To ask women to relinquish a right and a duty in exchange for a courtesy, is to ask them to do what is dishonorable. If voting be a right, yield it; if it be not a right, withhold it; but to acknowledge the right, and attempt to scare off or buy off the claimant, is a process not adapted to excite respect for the masculine character or confidence in the masculine wisdom.

If a man, robbed of his purse by a highwayman, or kept out of his rightful inheritance by an unscrupulous kinsman, should seek justice from the law, how would he like to be bidden by the judge, "Go home to your farm and your plough; there you will find enough to do. You will get far more money and respect by teaching your boys how to plant and hoe than you ever can by prosecuting lawsuits!" Nor would it tend to soothe his feelings that the judge were himself the highwayman. "I want justice," he would say, "not advice. Your suggestions are impertinent. Cease to wrong me before you dare counsel me." So may the women who claim rights say to the men who withhold them and counsel duties. This is not argument; it is insult. There can be no more brazen effrontery than for men to attempt to dictate to women their sphere. It is an assumption of Divine prerogative which can excite only anger and bitterness. It is this unwarranted and contemptuous dictation which gives to the woman's-rights struggle its animosity and repulsiveness. Women kept back from what they believe to be their own, from what they can show as good a title to as any man, are told to go home and do housework. All that there is of spirit in a woman rises up in defiance. What right have men to assume such judgeship? Who made them interpreter between God and woman? Her duty, her sphere, lies between herself and her Maker. What she can do, and what she chooses to do, she has a Divine right to do, subject only to Divine limitations. She is no more under bonds to do housework than is a man. If she chooses and has the ability to get her living in some other way, she has the same right to do it that a man has. A popular lecturer not long since declared that Anna Dickinson could make as good a loaf of bread as any one, and that there was nowhere a better-ordered cottage than that over which Lucy Stone presided. His motives were good, and his statements may have been adapted to the hardness of his hearers' hearts, but he should never have condescended to make them. It was coming down from the true position to pander to a false principle. So far as lecturer or audience was concerned, judging from the newspaper report of the lecture, it is no more Anna Dickinson's duty to know how to make bread than it is Caleb Cushing's. Whether Anna Dickinson can make bread, or Lucy Stone keep house, is the affair only of those persons for whom it is the duty of the one to make bread and of the other to keep house. If Anna Dickinson chooses to deliver lectures, and buy bread with the proceeds instead of making it,—if Lucy Stone and her husband choose that she shall deliver lectures and hire a pair of hands to keep their house,—it is altogether fitting and proper. It is a thousand times more fitting and proper a way of keeping house than the way which men not unfrequently adopt, and without rebuke,—namely, marrying for it. Let us see every man bound down to one specific trade before we attempt to bind woman. Let us see every boy constrained to raise wheat to make bread with, before we constrain every girl to make bread.

"The education of girls now-a-days is extremely absurd," an honorable gentleman is reported in the morning paper to have said at a meeting of the Social Science Association. "There is no sense in having girls study Greek and Latin when they cannot make good bread, pies, or puddings"; and every girl of character and individuality who read his words vowed in her heart eternal hostility to the making of bread, pies, and puddings, — a vow which she will faithfully keep till some strong influence comes upon her, and makes the distasteful work pleasant. But meanwhile the contemptuous words have borne fruit of indignation and disdain towards the speaker, when there might have been respect and docility. Why will men destroy the advantage which their education, their position, and their sex give them, by these foolish words? Why will they be so blind as not to see where the true mischief and danger lie? Why do not men say to women, and to those about to become women, what they might say with tenfold more effect than any woman's words would have,—why do they not say, instead of those debasing sensual teachings which make woman a mere waiter upon the gross necessities of man, and which are only more disastrous when they are accepted than when they are rejected,—why do they not say, "Be content to strive for nothing less than all which a woman may become. Cease to think that pettiness and frivolity and insipidity are feminine accomplishments. Cease to think it a beautiful, a graceful, a womanly thing to be a fool. Strengthen the mind by study and the body by exercise. Store your memory with facts, and cultivate your judgment by reasoning. Fit yourself for the place which you select or accept. Be wife, mother, teacher, nurse, what you will, but be your best; and be always a woman first; be always higher than your work. Remember always that you must be before you can do. Scorn to contract your powers to the narrow circle of your personal contact, but comprehend with your interest all that touches welfare. Consider nothing human as foreign to you. Make home, so far as you have or can have power, a centre of comfort indeed, but of light, of intelligence, of humanity as well, and count the whole country your home, and the whole world your country. Disdain to affect or to cherish an ignorant innocence, but wear an aggressive and all-conquering purity. Remember that the perfect woman is nobly planned, not only to warn and comfort, but to command. Learn to think nobly, to love nobly, to live nobly, and demand and enforce by your own nobility, from all who seek your friendship or companionship, the same outreach for noble thought and love and life."

Do men fancy that the sceptre will depart from them when women become sovereigns? So long as women remain subjects, the sceptre crumbles in man's grasp, and his kingdom runs to waste. It is not women alone who suffer from the ignorance and inability, not to say imbecility, which have been sedulously inculcated upon woman as a grace and a charm. Men come down to meet their women. It is wellnigh impossible for a man to live high when the women of his household and his acquaintance are constantly attracting him to live low. When women drivel, men grovel. If men really feel that they are too mean and feeble and false to retain their influence over women, when women shall be encouraged to a free and full development, there is a sort of wisdom in their small-talk of bread and butter. Happily there are men who have sufficient self-respect to look, not only without dismay, but with lively satisfaction, upon every sign of improvement in the character and education of women; who feel neither gratified nor conciliated to hear a woman declare that she cares nothing about politics and has all the rights she wants; men who are not deceived by the sentimentalisms of a threadbare chivalry, but who see and say that the influence of a large-natured woman is elevating, and the influence of a small-natured woman is degrading.

Breadth and depth of culture are the only royal road even to good housekeeping. Granted that the majority of women do lead a domestic life, and should therefore be educated with reference to it; there is no employment in the world that needs Greek and Latin more than domestic employment. The position of a woman at the head of a family is more like that of a man at the head of a government than like any other. Every possible variety of mental training she needs; every possible variety of intellectual furnishing will come into use. Without the liberality, the comprehensiveness, the wisdom, which education gives, she cannot administer the affairs of her kingdom well. Natural tact will do much, but it cannot supply the place of education. When a woman has learned to make a pudding, she has learned but the smallest and easiest part of her duty. She needs to know how to sit at the table where the pudding is served, and dispense a hospitality so cordial and enlivening that the pudding shall be forgotten. There are a thousand women who can make a pudding, where there is one who is mistress of her servants, of her children, of her husband, of her house, of her position. Granted that women need have no character on their own account,—that their glory and dignity and importance lie in being the mothers of men. All on that ground they need the most thorough intellectual education. A woman can make a dress fit well though she have little knowledge of anything else; but she cannot fashion an immortal soul for a worthy immortality without a worthy cultivation of her own soul. A woman who is not the equal of men is not fit to be the mother of men.

Let me nòt, however, miss an opportunity, or anything that may be construed into an opportunity, to repudiate this whole doctrine. A woman should be strong and wise and cultivated, not chiefly because she becomes thereby a better wife and mother, but because wisdom is better than folly, strength than weakness, cultivation than neglect. A woman's glory is in herself. If she is wise, she is wise for herself. It is just as great for her to do a great thing herself as it is to have her husband or son do it, and husband and son are all the more likely to be great for her grandeur. But what with pulpit and press, lecture-room and social science, the theory that woman is but a mere auxiliary of man seems to be reviving with great force. The Mohammedan and the Mormon doctrines are that women have no life in the next world except through their husbands. The Christian doctrine is that they have none in this. "Man," says a popular lecturer, "needs the conscious affection of a female heart to soften the asperities of his own, and to give completeness to his being." But what of the female heart while it is thus softening his asperities and completing his being? Is asperity-softening a pleasant work? Will it be likely to give completeness to the female being? or is she supposed to be already complete? "In order to found a home," says the same lecturer, according to the newspaper report, "the first thing to do is to look around for a woman who would make a good partner in this home business, — a woman pure, good, sensible, modest, tidy, good-looking, and intelligent." I should say, decidedly the first thing for him is to take a good long look at himself, and make sure that he is pure, good, sensible, modest, tidy, good-looking, and intelligent, and therefore a fit person for a woman of such qualities to associate with. "Her support, her dignity, her beauty, her honor and happiness, lie in her dependence as wife, mother, and daughter. . . . . The woman who, at this day, feels that to be the mother of living children is the first, highest . . . . lot, is worthy of all admiration and praise." What góspel is this? Honor and dignity and happiness consist not in truth, integrity, self-sacrifice, self-command, benevolence, communion with God, and likeness to Christ, but in marriage and motherhood and housekeeping! Where is the warrant for such affirmations? Not surely in the words of the Master. Christ propounded no such doctrines. He had many and devoted friends among women. He spoke to women and of women in public and private. He gave them instruction, advice, and consolation. His tenderness towards them was so manly, so divine, that even now, dimly seen through lengthening years, imperfectly told in a strange tongue, it falls upon the heart like dew; but never a word he spake that the most perverse ingenuity could wrest to the support of this unregenerate theory. He never so branded woman with the mark of the beast. So far as his words have any bearing upon it, they bear against it. He looked upon woman, he treated woman, as a human being. Nothing that he ever said could be construed into a concession of her inferiority to man. He gave her equal respect, less rebuke. His denunciations of men were sometimes terrible. He never spoke a harsh word to a woman. Paul, in the glow of inspiration, uttering truths which span the whole heaven of the soul, nevertheless sometimes showed in his teachings the influence of his age. Christ shone, mildly to meet our darkened eyes, above all ages. Paul could never quite get out of his mind the notion of woman's sphere. Into the mind of Christ it never came. Paul admonished women to guide the house. Jesus applauded a woman for not guiding the house. All his intercourse with woman was adapted to lift her up from the level where she stood into a higher region, — to take her above the wearying, petty cares of "her sphere," and fix her thoughts on higher themes, — themes that expand the mind and enlarge the heart. It was not Martha, cumbered with much serving, but Mary, who left her house to look after itself while she sat at Jesus' feet, who received his commendation. Martha is the model woman of men, but Jesus praised Mary. Men at different times brought accusations against women, but Jesus always maintained their cause. Even when they were palpably and grievously wrong, he shielded their guilt with his own purity, and couched his censure in such gentleness that displeasure is swallowed up in love. O, never man spake like this man!

I wish our grave and reverend teachers could know how deep, how thorough, how abiding is the repugnance felt by every woman not debased by corrupt male influence towards those who, instead of teaching men to be so pure and high-minded as to be worthy of becoming husbands and fathers, spend their strength in inculcating upon women the duty of becoming wives and mothers, enforcing that by argument which should only be won by grace, degrading into a means of coarse material prosperity that which is meant to minister the finest spiritual succor, till all the sacraments of life seem likely to be swept away.

How long shall men attempt to steady the ark of the Lord by putting forth upon it their own unconsecrated hands?

How many generations must die before we learn that the Lord is in his holy temple, and that the only fitting worship is for all the earth to keep silence before him? Whenever there are confusion and disaster, it is because the people have gone aside after Baalim and Ashtaroth. The gospel of material prosperity is very little higher than no gospel at all. It never can heal the hurt of the daughter of my people.

How swiftly, harmoniously, and completely, during the late war, did the relations between men and women adjust themselves! The whole country was flooded with a sudden outburst of love, — love of country, of freedom, and of right. There was no quarrelling as to who was head and who was heart. Instinctively, head and heart worked together. In the Sanitary Commission rooms, in the hospitals, in camps, on battlefields, at the mammoth fairs, men and women wrought side by side, the great hearts of both sexes bearing down all the clamors of incompetence, and petty, brief authority, and never clashing with each other. Men and women ordered, organized, and obeyed, as instinct and fitness prompted. Their "spheres" cut across one another without the slightest regard to, or the smallest hindrance from, tradition. The "Boys in Blue," a book which almost revives again the sacred fury of those glorious days, shows again and again how utterly false and futile are the old dogmas of woman's sphere,—how quickly they shrivel in the ardor of a purpose or a passion,—how woman's sphere comprises everything that needs to be done and that she can do. Men went out to fight, and women went out to heal; and the fighting men became women in weakness and tenderness and gratitude and love; and the healing women became men in strength and support and consolation; and both were never more divinely themselves. Let me give from many stories one, — the story of Mother Bickerdyke.

"'Mother' was the sobriquet of this extraordinary woman throughout the entire Western army. In General Sherman's old corps (the Fifteenth) she seemed to be the individual mother of every man in the ranks. The prairie-plough and the thunder-storm were needed, and they came in the person of Mrs. Bickerdyke. A pythoness if her precious boys, as she called them, were assaulted, she was gentle and tender as a loving mother to every sick and wounded soldier. Woe be to the man, no matter what his rank, who trampled on the rights of the 'boys in blue.' Faithful surgeons praised her, and relied upon her skill, strength, and tenderness. Those who were the reverse cursed her, and clamored for her removal. . . . . Her efforts not only saved unnumbered lives and mitigated untold sufferings in her own hospitals, but, by the example they afforded to others, became schools of instruction. Her huge organized laundries saved hundreds of thousands of dollars to the government and to the Sanitary Commission, by washing what would otherwise have been destroyed, to say nothing of the health and comfort they bestowed upon the sick. She was herculean in strength, and indomitable in will, and possessed the most extraordinary endurance. She saw no lions in the way, admitted the existence of no obstacles,— naming what others would regard as such 'cobwebs,'— and these she demolished with nonchalant and invincible energy. The surgeons admitted that she had no rival in extemporizing, organizing, and running hospitals. . . . . The great military men — Grant, Sherman, McPherson, Thomas, Logan — were her firm friends, and supplied her with facilities to carry on her work. . . . . She soon discovered a disposition to misappropriate sanitary stores, and raised her first *tempest* in the Brick Hospital at Cairo. A fine box of supplies had been consigned to her at Galesburg, conspicuously marked with the name of the society that sent them. She gave a certain number of shirts, socks, and slippers to a ward-master to distribute. The next morning, in going her rounds, she perceived this official wearing a Sanitary shirt, broadly marked, while one of his sick patients was minus his clean one. 'Where did you get that shirt?' she said fiercely. 'It 's none of your business,' he answered. 'I 'll see if it is n't,' she replied; and seizing it, as he had no coat on, she drew it over the head of the unfortunate wight, stunned into silence. 'Now let me see your feet,' said she, stooping and taking one in her hand. Off came the socks and slippers in a twinkling, to the infinite delight of the patients. The denuded thief slunk off suddenly, a sadder and a wiser man, and Mrs. B. had no further trouble in this hospital concerning Sanitary stores. . . . . She was matron of the large and complete hospital at Corinth, which occupied the female academy of that place, beautifully situated on rising ground, with a large addition of hospital tents. She had established in the building a fine diet kitchen and laundry, and was running the entire concern with her customary success, when the battle commenced, and was fought, on the 3d and 4th of October, 1862. So perfect and comprehensive was the system, that, notwithstanding the immense and sudden influx of wounded during the battle, and sick and wounded Rebels left on our hands at its conclusion, it was said that perfect order was maintained, and every man attended properly. . . . . The medical staff were in a spasm of delight over a feat she had just accomplished. The small-pox hospital had become a charnel-house, and there seemed none to regenerate it. . . . . She at once took charge of the revolting place. An ordinary thunder-storm would be powerless here, and she created an earthquake; ran the prairie-plough through the filthy grounds and out-houses, overturning cots, and . . . . in three weeks had a pure, clean hospital, where few men died, and all were made as comfortable as the loathsome disease would permit. . . . . In the spring of 1864 she came North to carry out a characteristic Bickerdyke project. She declared the boys in hospital *must* have fresh milk, and nothing but cows could give it; and they *must* be solicited from the Western farmers, and taken down to Memphis. And then she wanted hundreds of hens to lay fresh eggs for the sick. The Commission consented to the plan, and agreed to furnish transportation for the cows and hens. . . . . Mrs. B. procured eighty cows and several hundred hens, and they were transmitted to her at Memphis. . . . . She remained with Sherman's army through the entire series of its brilliant victories and bloody fights, receiving and caring for its wounded, running and consolidating hospitals, superintending laundries. . . . . She superintended the cooking of hundreds of tons of sanitary stores and vegetables. . . . . If in her journeys she found men suffering with wounds festering for lack of clean bandages, her own clothing was torn into strips, and her own night-dresses taken for clean covering for the poor emaciated soldiers. .... No exigencies baffled her skill and self-denial."

I should like to see Dr. Todd tiptoeing up to Mother Bickerdyke and telling her that her happiness consisted in her dependence as wife, mother, and daughter!

Was she an exception to the general rule? Were the thousands upon thousands of women who worked in the ranks of this great army of healers exceptions? And were the men who worked with them and found them helpers exceptions?

We cannot always have a war in which to fuse our prejudices and puerilities, but we might learn from our experience during this one war that wifehood and motherhood are set within no narrow bounds, depend upon no external conditions, but spring from the heart, inhere in the nature. With all this glowing past just behind us, how can men stand up and preach their trivialities? Seeing how mightily and steadfastly love wrought through those bloody years, why do they not bring love to the solution of the problem now? If it could heal the wounds of war, why can it not heal the wounds of peace? Why fumble about among earth-forces and leave out of the reckoning the one force of Heaven, stronger than all? Is motherhood ceasing to be honored? It is because you have robbed it of its honor, you have plundered it of its element from heaven, and left only the base residuum of earth. Restore to it that which alone can give it sweetness. Only love and hope and joy wait upon the offspring of love and hope and joy, and the soul that springs from any other source is itself a monstrosity,—the guilt and shame of the authors of its being.

To be a mother is of itself neither

great nor high. It furnishes the opportunity for much loving and large living, but in itself it is neither the one nor the other. Mere natural maternity is a fact of no moral significance whatever. The best mother shares it in common with the worst, and with all the lower creation. It does not necessarily even improve the character. It may be absolutely bare of virtue and of grace. It may spring from vice and crime, and end in shame and woe. To give life to a sentient being, without being able to make provision to turn life to the best account, — to give life, careless whether it will be bale or boon to the recipient, — is the sin of sins. Every other sin mars what it finds. This makes what it mars.

A motherhood that exalts the nature, that brings the soul closer to all humanity, and so interprets to it God, is worshipful indeed. A motherhood petty and selfish, narrowing itself down to meet only the demands and discern only the excellences of its own offspring, separating itself from, instead of allying itself to, its kind, is evil, and that continually.

There is more to be learned of the true spirit, the ultimate import of marriage, from the co-operation of man and woman in the late war, than from all the elaborate discourses through which it has been trailed; for marriage is a friendship of the sexes so profound, so comprehensive, that it includes the whole being. The inflow of the divine life,

> "Bright effluence of bright essence increate,"

blends the man nature and the woman nature into an absolute oneness, which shapes itself ever thereafter into the only perfect symmetry. Thus alone comes humanity in the unity of the faith, and of the knowledge of the Son of God, unto a perfect man, unto the measure of the stature of the fulness of Christ. Thus marriage forever tends to its own annihilation, — not the annihilation of a stream swallowed up in desert sands, but of a river broadening to the boundless sea. The more perfect its substance the more yielding its form. As it gathers power it diminishes pomp, till, by a pathway which the vulture's eye hath not seen and never can see, marriage itself leads to the land where they neither marry nor are given in marriage.

Wherever man pays reverence to woman, — wherever any man feels the influence of any woman, purifying, chastening, abashing, strengthening him against temptation, shielding him from evil, ministering to his self-respect, medicining his weariness, peopling his solitude, winning him from sordid prizes, enlivening his monotonous days with mirth, or fancy, or wit, flashing heaven upon his earth, and mellowing it for all spiritual fertility,—there is the element of marriage. Wherever woman pays reverence to man,—wherever any woman rejoices in the strength of any man, feels it to be God's agent, upholding her weakness, confirming her purpose, and crowning her power,—wherever he reveals himself to her, just, upright, inflexible, yet tolerant, merciful, benignant, not unruffled, perhaps, but not overcome by the world's turbulence, and responding to all her gentleness, his feet on the earth, his head among the stars, helping her to hold her soul steadfast in right, to stand firm against the encroachments of frivolity, vanity, impatience, fatigue, and discouragement, helping to preserve her good-nature, to develop her energy, to consolidate her thought, to utilize her benevolence, to exalt and illumine her life,—there is the essence of marriage.

Its love is founded on respect, and increases self-respect at the very moment of merging self in another. Its love is mutual, equally giving and receiving at every instant of its action. There is neither dependence nor independence, but inter-dependence. Years cannot weaken its bonds, distance cannot sunder them. It is a love which vanquishes the grave, and transfigures death itself into life.

The current of human progress is undoubtedly — perhaps has always been — setting in this direction. Its motion is slow, sometimes apparently backward, but never permanently checked. Every legal enactment that tends to equalize the sexes, to give husband and wife the same position before the law, smooths the way for the desired end. Every elevated friendship between a man and a woman prefigures it. All the subjugations of the marriage rite and of common law are against it. Everything which coerces that whose only value lies in its freedom is an obstruction. So long as the law commands subordination, it forbids the grace of a spontaneous deference. Man never will be truly monarch, till woman of her own will places the crown on his brow; and that she will never do till her will is free. Each being in a false relation to the other, there will be constant antagonism where there ought to be unbroken harmony. They will hinder and irritate where they ought to help and soothe. Man may have mastery by strength of thew and sinew; but he masters only thew and sinew. The fine spirit escapes him. The subtile soul, bruised, outraged, deformed, but defiant, mocks him from afar.

So long as the tendencies of growth,

however feeble and awry, are to fill out the empty shell of marriage with true spiritual richness, we may hold our peace. But when our preachers and teachers come to us and set down this empty shell square in the path of progress, and say, "This is all, — all that has been, all that shall be, all that God intended ever should be," the stones may cry out upon them. It is the very priests thrusting God from his most holy temple. It is the ministers of that Gospel which emancipates woman from centuries of servility, remanding her to her burdens. Christ made no distinction, but opened the door wide to woman as to man. These restrict her to a single form of service, while oppressing her with a thousand forms of servitude. They subordinate her best uses to her lowest functions. They degrade her into a hewer of wood and a drawer of water, and add blasphemy to falsehood with a "thus saith the Lord."

And yet men in their errors are not wholly without excuse. They have a dim sense of the truth uttered, yet hardly revealed, in the Hebrew Scriptures, that man was formed of the dust of the ground, but woman was formed of man. His origin is the dull insensate clod; hers, the clod already vivified and humanized. The material for his workmanship is pre-eminently the earth, hers humanity. His diamond is in the rough, hers has already taken its first polish.

Men, in their reiterated and wearisome injunctions to women to be wives, mothers, and housekeepers, are following, after a stumbling and uncertain fashion, the glimmer of this truth. Feeling, in some blind, instinctive sort, that woman's work is other and higher than theirs, they know no better way to further it than to bind manacles on her wrists, and set her to doing what they interpret to be her divinely appointed task. Women will but fall into the corresponding error, if in the release from restraint they forget for a time that for them all forced physical labor is but the least of many evils. It is better to dig than to beg; but it is only a fatal misunderstanding of needs, and a most extravagant misapplication of forces, that reduces woman to the alternative of digging or begging. Any coarse manual work is better than idleness; but it is only because we have as yet so little knowledge of real social science that any woman is doomed to coarse manual work as a refuge from idleness. The fields which women alone can reap are white already to harvest; the laborers are few, because society is not yet clear-eyed enough to see the fruit that ripens there. Men do not know there is any such harvest. The very fields are to them but "fenceless fields of air." So the hands that were divinely fashioned for this doing are set to unhandsome service. Woman is largely occupied with man's work. In the sweat of her face she eats bread. It is like taking a Damascus blade to hew timber withal. Never can she do her own work till man lifts from her shoulders the burden that belongs to his. A large part of the labor which he assigns her as from God is as really foreign to her "sphere" as the field-work which he denounces. It matters not whether woman be out of doors or in; hanging on yard-arms or bending over a cooking-stove. All wearing physical labor is unsuited to her. All enforced muscular work beyond what is necessary to her own symmetrical development is the result of defective human arrangement, not of perfect Divine establishment. Yet, with all their talk, so unconscious are men of woman's true work, that when you take away all that does not belong to it, all which is a hindrance to it, most of them will think you have left only idleness. Their eyes are holden that they do not see. It is so impalpable, so intangible to everything but instinct, that it defies delineation. It is as pervasive, but also as evasive, as religion. Its conditions are comfort, freedom, serenity. Its antagonists are toil, weariness, anxiety. Its right is to be ministered unto in carnal things; its province is to minister in spiritual things. But it is dumb. It has no voice. It accomplishes all things in silence, choosing rather to die than give a sign. Motherliness may best express its source, but it is motherliness, not as a biographical incident, but as an essential attribute. Let the mother's character, the mother's work, be the true character and work of woman; but not that narrow kind held within the mere literal words. That is but a type, a symbol. Wherever there is weakness to be succored, hurt to be healed, good to be done, grace to be shown, there is mother's love to lavish, there is mother's work to do. The ideal woman feels that all the children of want, — bodily, mental, moral want, the infant of days or the man bowed with age, — all are children whom the Lord has given her, and over a wide and ever-widening circle beams the radiance of her spotless motherhood. If she has not first created the claims which she satisfies, if she has not herself evoked the responsibilities which she discharges, she does but diffuse, without diminishing, the love which would otherwise have been concentrated. She misses the narrower, only to find the larger life. She looks to no future reaping as a reward for her sowing, counts upon no material revenue, but finds her delight in her doing, and gathers, as she goes, abundant spiritual harvests. Thanks, gratitude, admiration, are but the tithe of her meed. That feeble hands stretch out imploringly to her, that blind eyes turn wistfully whenever her footfall sounds, that fainting hearts and bounding hearts rely instinctively on her sympathy, — this is her constant, silent blessedness. Her world may be large or small, but she is mother of its best manhood. She calls forth whatever is pure, noble, tender, whatever is manliest in man. Evil shrinks away abashed before her steps. Discord attunes itself to melody charmed by the music of her voice. Women thrill to her revelation of their own highest nature. Men yield enraptured to the spell of her sweet unlikeness. In the large helpfulness, the irresistible attraction of her life, she bodies forth all that woman will be to man, all that man will receive from woman, all the honor wherewith he shall crown her in the day of their yet distant espousals.

THE END.

Cambridge: Stereotyped and Printed by Welch, Bigelow, & Co.

www.ingramcontent.com/pod-product-compliance
Lightning Source LLC
LaVergne TN
LVHW011210110826
845150LV00006B/1392

9781425517625